TOM FONTAINE'S RARE LIFETIME COLLECTIONS PRESENTS ...

SHARON TATE
Every Picture Tells Her Story

Copyright ©2025, The Fontaine Collection

ALL RIGHTS RESERVED.

No part of this publication may be reproduced, stored in a retrieval system, or transmitted in any form or by any means—electronic, mechanical, photocopy, recording, or any other—except for brief quotation in reviews, without the prior permission of the author or publisher.

ISBN: 978-1-962402-10-1

Photography by Michelle Pemberton and Tom and Mary Fontaine
All Images and Illustrations provided by The Fontaine Collection
Book layout and design by Tom Fontaine and Robin Surface

Image Credits

Cover photo and page 71: 101321403 © publicdomainstockphotos | Dreamstime.com; page 3: 1961 Columbia High School yearbook; page 13, 8x10 promotional photo*; page 29: *Eye Of the Devil* 8x10 lobby still*; page 39: *Fearless Vampire Killers* French lobby card*; page 51: candid photos*; page 56: original negative of Sharon Tate*; page 54, 55, candid photos *; page 57, 58, and 59 candid photos *page 61: *Don't Make Waves* VHS Box*; page 89: *Valley of The Dolls* 8x10 lobby still*; page 109: *Wrecking Crew* 8x10 lobby still*; page 121: 100875613 © publicdomainstockphotos | Dreamstime.com; page 133: *12+1* lobby card*; page 143: 2 original negatives*

*Indicates my collection as shown

Published by

This book is dedicated to

my wife Mary,

my brother Mark

and to the memory of my parents,

Thomas and Josephine, for the love and support

I have been given for over fifty years that allowed me

to follow my dreams and my passion

in whatever I have chosen to pursue.

For Sharon

Table of Contents

Introduction 1

The Early Years 5

She Is On Her Way (the TV Years) 13

Odele De Caray *(Eye of the Devil)* 29

Sarah Shagal *(The Fearless Vampire Killers)* 39

Jay & Roman 51

Malibu *(Don't Make Waves)* 61

Fashion (Sharon's Personally Owned) 71

Jennifer North *(Valley of the Dolls)* 89

Freya Carlson *(The Wrecking Crew)* 109

Art and Publicaions 121

Pat *(12 + 1)* 133

Friends 143

1969/Once Upon a Time 153

Introduction

As 1968 started, not knowing what this year would mean in history, I discovered a name that would stay with me forever, Sharon Tate. How did this all occur? My father, a big influence on me in every way, told me about her when I was nine years old. And just like every other important thing he talked to me about, I never forgot it. Thanks Dad!

In the winter of 1967, my Dad and Del Medlock, our neighbor and friend, went to see a movie. In those days that was a common occurrence as the only other entertainment we had was a black and white TV with four channels and the radio. Hard to believe, but it was true. When he came home from that movie, I asked him what he saw and he told me *Valley of the Dolls*. It wasn't really the movie that blew him away though, it was a certain actress who mesmerized him and Del each time she appeared on the screen. I asked innocently who this actress was, and he said her name was Sharon Tate and she played Jennifer in the movie. As a curious youngster, who was already in my fourth year as a collector, I asked in a naive way why he liked her so much. He simply stated, "She's stunningly beautiful! I could not keep my eyes off her when she was on the screen." He went on to comment that the rest of the movie was just okay in his opinion. He'd gone to see it because it was "the movie" to see at the time, and had received a lot of publicity because it was based on Jacqueline Suzann's bestselling book. My Dad stated unequivocally, "Sharon Tate is going to be a famous star."

Well that did it for me — if my Dad liked her she had to be someone special. I had to find out more about this new up-and-coming star. So, on Saturdays I went down to my local drugstore and spent a lot of time looking at movie magazines to educate myself. I soon found out she was doing a new movie with my favorite actor, Dean Martin who would play a secret agent named Matt Helm. In my continuing research, I found out she had made another movie titled *Don't Make Waves*, co-starring with my second favorite actor, Tony Curtis. I now knew for sure that Sharon was someone special. She would soon become famous as the new "it" girl and make a name for herself in Hollywood. Living in the Midwest as I did, I continued to get to know her by keeping up with the movie magazines. She seemed to have everything going for her, but it all changed on August 9, 1969, just eight days after my eleventh birthday. Like many people, I was saddened by the loss and have always had a special place in my heart for Sharon.

I kept these thoughts of Sharon and my collection private but I always had a dream that I could one day have an exhibit celebrating her life out west. I even spoke with Patty Duke and Barbara Parkins, her co-stars from *Valley of the Dolls*, at a Hollywood Collector Show several years ago and shared my ideas with them. Barbara was on board after I told her it was about Sharon's life, not what happened. Patty also agreed but has since left us. So, my dream was set aside.

At the age of 64, I felt it was time to feature Sharon's story using my collection as sort of a visual biography. Her story has been told many times in many ways, but none were quite like this. I hope you enjoy seeing these incredible artifacts, some for the very first time. This truly was a labor of love celebrating Sharon's life, and closing a special chapter in mine.

Tom Fontaine

October 2022

The Early Years

When I was in school,
I dreamed about becoming a psychiatrist or a ballerina.
Like most girls I would dream about being a movie star too.

– Sharon Tate
As quoted in Screen Stories *magazine (1967)*

Sharon Tate —The Early Years

Sharon Tate was born on January 24, 1943, in Dallas, Texas. She was a shy, bashful girl. Her parents, Paul and Doris, were strict with her but did not stop her from going into modeling at a very young age.

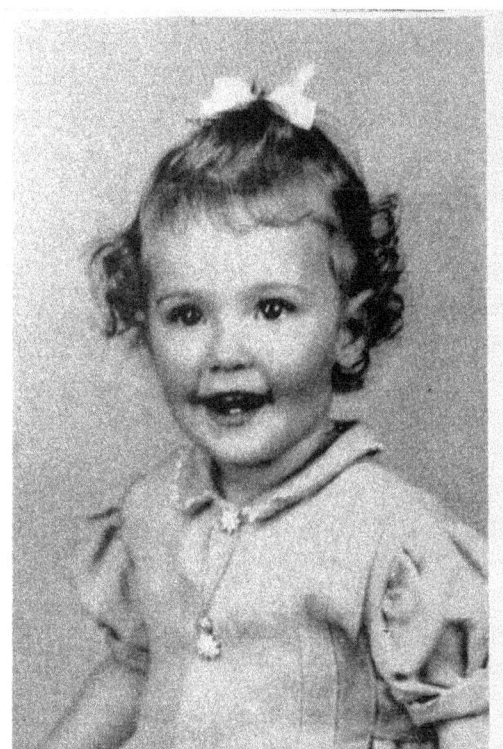
At 6 months Sharon won Dallas' "Miss Tiny Tot" award.

She won her first beauty pageant, Miss Tiny Tot of Dallas, when she was six months old, and won five other beauty pageants during 1959, when she was 16 years old: Miss Richland, Miss Tri-Cities, Miss Autorama, Miss Frontier Days, and Miss Water Follies.

Sharon spent the first part of her childhood in Texas, but because her Father was in the military Sharon, who considered herself a military brat, traveled wherever Paul was transferred. All the traveling made it hard for Sharon to have friends, but a led to a tight bond with her two sisters, Patti and Debra.

She ended up in Richland, Washington during her high school years. She was crowned Sophomore Princess of Columbia High School in 1958. She eventually landed back in Texas her Junior year of high school and finally relocated to Vicenza, Italy, where she was Homecoming Queen and Senior

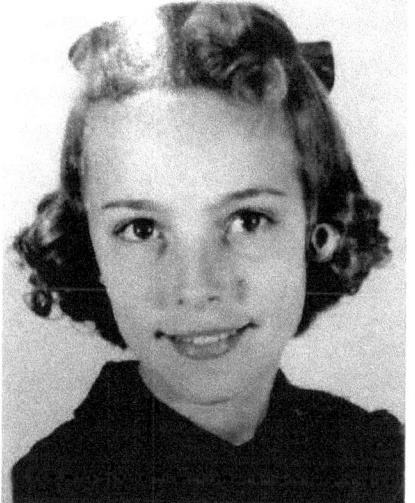

Prom Queen before she graduated. She was well-educated and spoke Italian.

Yes, Sharon was beautiful, but she also achieved many things with her athletic abilities. She was a star basketball player, cheerleader, student council member and was very popular in all her schools in the United States and Italy. She starred as Juliet in her high school's production of *Romeo & Juliet.* With all of this recognition and encouragement behind her, it's no surprise that Tate built the confidence to continue to pursue an acting career as she got older. It seemed like everyone knew she was one of a kind and something special.

Sharon's Handwritten Letter to Her Grandmother, 1959

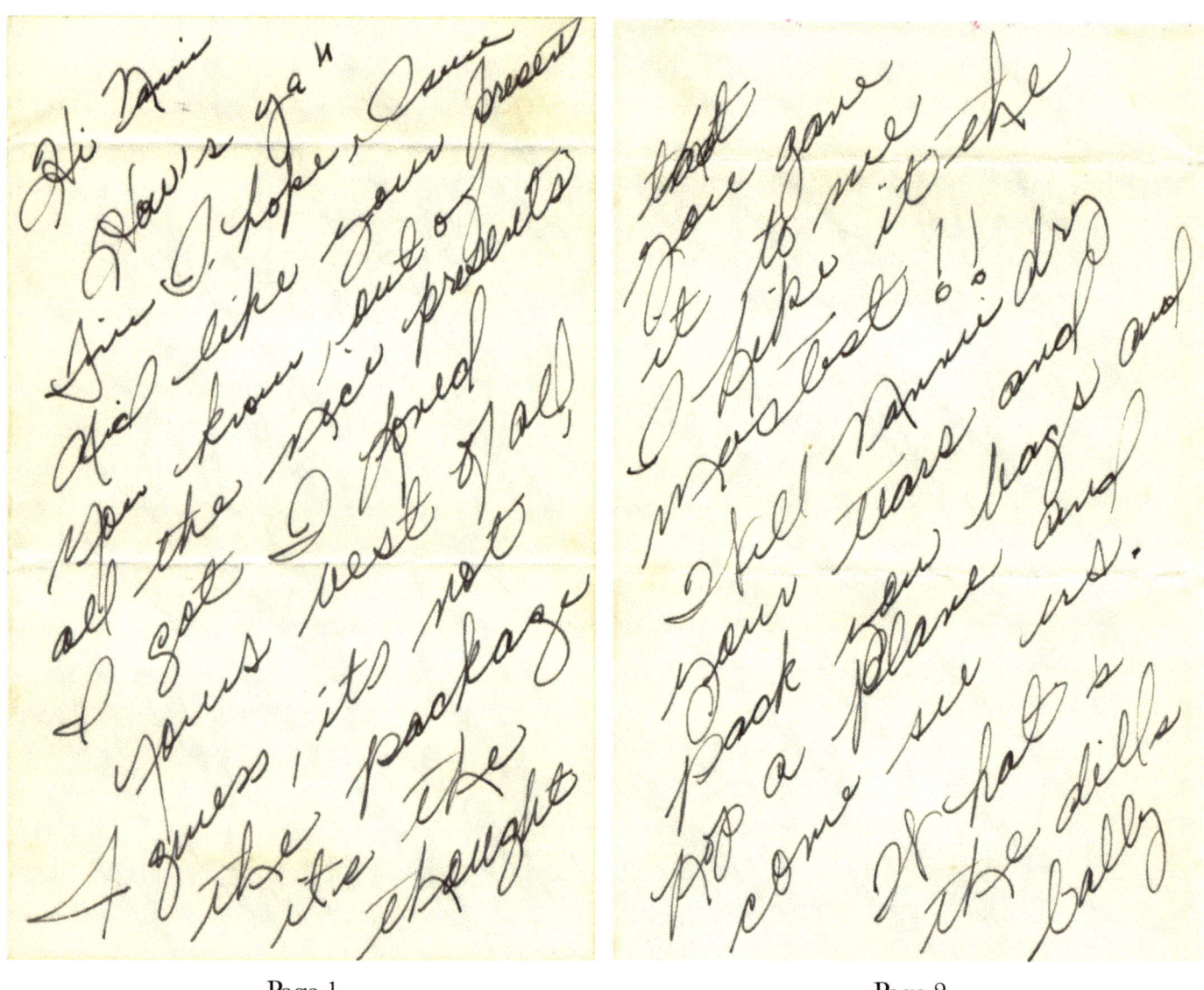

Page 1

Hi Nan,
How's ya"
Fine I hope. Sure
did like your present
You know, out of
all the nice presents
I got I loved
yours best of all,
I guess, it's not
like the package
it's the
thought

Page 2

that
have gone
it to me
I like it the
mostest !!
Tell Nannie dry
your tears and
pack your bags and
hop a plane and
come see us.
That's
the dills
bally

look? is
she cute?
I sure feel
they are proud
of her, Oh you cousin
Jane are mother coll-
to cold to our coll-
lation don't tell?"
Nell had
at her close
now her
time big

Kiss
for me &
everyone too.
Will See
Soon.

Love &
Stuff
devoted
Grand
Child

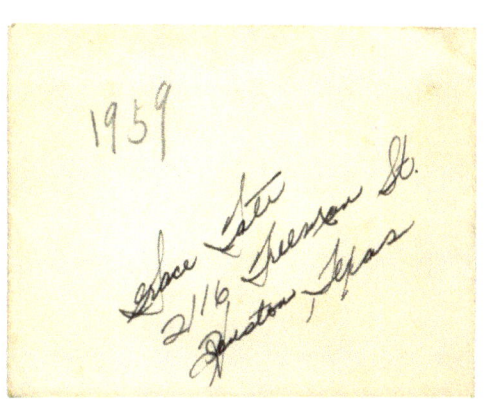

1959

Grace Tate
2116 Tierson St.
Houston, Texas

3-19-61
The only letter I
ever had from
Sharon

School Days

Sharon attended several grade schools and high schools all over the world as she and her family relocated where her father, a Captain in the Army, was stationed. She attended Columbia High School, now known as Richland High School, in Richland, Washington, from September 1958 to October 1959. She was voted Miss Richland in 1958.

Sharon attended Irvin High School in El Paso, Texas, for her Junior year (late fall of 1959).

Sherry Noland, Etah McCoy, and Sharon Tate anxiously await their fates at the high senior slave sale.

the orbit

juniors

Sears Sutton
Bill Swain
Russell Talbert
Sharon Tate
Ronald Taylor

Sharon's father was reassigned to Verona, Italy, in 1960, so the family moved there. She attended Vicenza American High School in Vicenza, Italy, from April 1960 to June 1961, and graduated from there in 1961.

SHARON TATE

HOMECOMING QUEEN

The highlight of our football season this year was the choice of lovely senior Sharon Tate as our first homecoming queen, thus beginning a new tradition in Vicenza High School. Chosen by the football team, Sharon represents our undefeated season.

*I'm thankful for my strict upbringing;
I feel it has helped me learn discipline –
and that's very important in this business.*

– Sharon Tate

As quoted in *Screen Stories* magazine (1967)

She Is On Her Way

*"My whole life has been decided by fate.
I've never planned anything that's happened to me."*
– Sharon Tate

The Struggle for Stardom in the Movies

In the early days of her career Sharon appeared in movies and unfortunately her scenes were very quick and never filmed but she was contracted. In my opinion it was a mistake as she was made for the camera with her stunning beauty.

After finishing high school in 1961 in Vicenza, Italy, Sharon was cast as an extra in the movie Barabbas also filmed in Italy and released in 1961. She was a Patrician in the Arena. You see Sharon briefly as she appears screaming along with the others in the crowd, although her appearance is uncredited. She did a screen test for the film, but unfortunately nothing came of it

Sharon makes a quick walk-on in *The Americanization of Emily,* released in 1964, but she was uncredited. Her manager, Martin Ransohoff set up a screen test for the role of Liesl, the eldest von Trapp daughter, in *The Sound of Music* in the fall of that year; however, the roll was given to Charmian Carr. This was a busy time for Sharon, but yielded no real results for her career.

In September (1963), Ransohoff finally began filming on The Sandpiper with Elizabeth Taylor and Richard Burton. It was delayed due to casting problems with Taylor. Things got even worse for Ransahoff because he gave Sharon a small part in the film. She never did a scene though, because she was ordered off the set by Taylor, who did not want to be up-staged by a 21 year old.

The Sandpiper was released in 1965 and Sharon attended the premiere as a show of respect for Ransahoff.

Now that is class!!

Sheet music from The Sandpiper *signed by Martin Ransohoff.*

In October she did a screen test for *The Cincinnati Kid*, another of Ransohoff's productions. This was an important screen test, as it was opposite Steve McQueen, who later became close friends with Sharon and Roman. She may have lost the part to Tuesday Weld, but she earned a great deal from McQueen and, more importantly, made a life-long friend.

Tarzan and the Valley of Gold

Like *Petticoat Junction* in her TV years, Sharon was the original casting pick for the female lead for the film *Tarzan and the Valley of Gold*, co-starting Mike Henry, a former football player. This was his first film. Martin Ransohoff, who had Sharon under exclusive contract, changed his mind about making this her film debut, and the role was later recast with Nancy Kovak, who later that year co-starred with Elvis Presley in *Frankie and Johnny*. This ended up being a blessing in disguise for Sharon, as the film got mixed reviews. Only pre-filming publicity photos for newspaper print/wire photos, etc. of Henry and Sharon exist for this film. No filming was done with both actors together.

Autograph of Steve McQueen with Sharon's autograph on the reverse side.

Original Wire/Newspaper publicity photo for Tarzan and the Valley of Gold *with Sharon and co-star Mike Henry. This is the only photo taken of the two before production started.*

The Television Years (1963–1969)

In February 1963, Sharon met actor Richard Beymer in Rome when he was filming a movie with Paul Newman. Beymer, who had portrayed Tony in *West Side Story* in 1961, and Sharon became close and he told Sharon that if she wanted to become an actress she would need an agent. He recommended his agent, Harold Gefsky. So at the age of 20, Sharon embarked on a career in Hollywood and met with Gefsky.

Even though she had very little acting experience, he signed her to a one year contract after their first meeting. That same day, he sent her for an audition in Hollywood. This is also at the time through Gefsky she was introduced to Filmways Inc. founder and producer Martin Ransohoff, who also produced motion pictures. He was also taken with Sharon and said to her, "Baby, we're going to make you a star."

He wanted her start slowly, however, since she really had no experience with acting. He wanted her to polish up her talent by appearing in television shows for Filmways. Though she would have a long-term relationship with Ransahoff, she and Gefsky mutually parted ways. Their agreement was terminated on March 10, 1965. She then signed with the William Morris Agency.

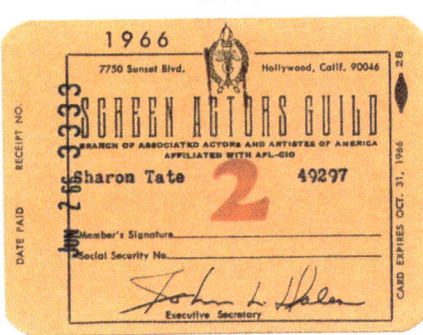

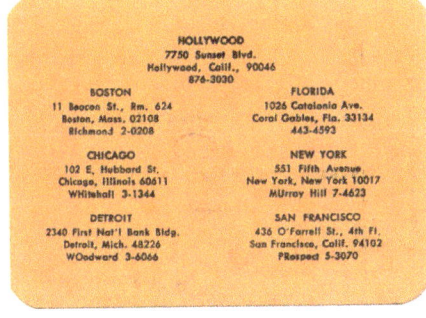

Sharon's Screen Actors Guild Card for 1966, along with her booklet with Marty Ransohoff's contact information handwritten by Sharon.

Sharon's original signed two-page contract parting ways with Harold Gefsky on March 10, 1965 to join the William Morris Agency

AGREEMENT between William Morris Agency, Inc. hereinafter referred to as "Morris", and Harold L. Gefsky Agency, hereinafter referred to as "Gefsky".

WITNESSETH

1. The parties contracting do so with reference to the following facts:

(a) Sharon Tate, hereinafter for convenience referred to as "Tate, employed Gefsky as an agent pursuant to SAG Theatrical Motion Picture, SAG-Television Motion Picture and AFTRA agency contracts dated January 27, 1965.

(b) Gefsky when acting as Tate's agent negotiated and obtained for Tate a contract of employment with Filmways of California, Inc. dated April 1, 1963.

(c) In accordance with Tate's request said agency contracts with Gefsky have been terminated and mutual releases have been granted by Gefsky and Tate with respect thereto.

(d) Tate subsequently employed Morris to act as her agent in the fields referred to in Paragraph 1(a) hereof and additionally in connection with the AGVA, Equity, General Services and General Materials & Packages fields for a period of three (3) years.

2. Morris agrees to pay to Gefsky the following:

(a) One-half of the commissions paid to Morris by Tate, as and when such commissions are actually received by Morris for engagements performed during the three year term of said agency contracts as referred to in Paragraph 1(d) hereof.

(b) One-fourth of the commissions paid to Morris by Tate, as and when such commissions are actually received by Morris, in connection with contracts or engagements entered into for Tate during the three year term of said agency contracts, but performed by Tate after the expiration of said three year term.

(c) With respect to package shows represented by Morris, the following shall apply: (1) In the event Tate enters into a contract for her services as a regular performer in a series, represented by Morris as the package agent, then to the extent Morris would be entitled to receive commission from Tate under SAG Agency regulations in such contract connection with. If Morris was not the package agent for such series, Morris shall pay to Gefsky, as and when package commissions are actually received by Morris for the applicable run, 5% or 2½% whichever is applicable, of the compensation actually paid to Tate in connection with such contract; (2) Except as expressly provided in (1), Morris is not obligated to pay, nor is Gefsky entitled to receive, any part of commissions payable to Morris in connection with package shows represented by Morris in which Tate may appear.

(d) Morris shall not be obligated to pay to Gefsky, nor shall Gefsky be entitled to receive any share of commissions paid to Morris by Tate in connection with any contracts or engagements entered into by Tate after the expiration of said three year term of the agency contracts between Morris and Tate as referred to in Paragraph 1(d) hereof.

(e) Notwithstanding anything hereinabove contained Gefsky shall be entitled to receive and retain for his own use and benefit the full commission on the earnings of Tate under and pursuant to her presently existing contract with Filmways of California, Inc. However, in the event during the three year term of said agency contracts Tate's contract with Filmways of California, Inc. is re-negotiated or improved, whether by way of an increase of the compensation set forth in her presently existing agreement with them, or by any way of a bonus, or otherwise, then, and in such event Morris shall be entitled to receive commission on the excess moneys received, and shall pay to Gefsky the applicable percentage, if any, of such commission, as provided for in sub-paragraph (a) and (b) of this Paragraph 2.

(f) In the event Morris becomes obligated to pay any other agent a share of Morris' commission of any employment Tate, then Gefsky's share shall be computed only on the balance left to and received by Morris.

3. It is expressly understood and agreed that the execution of this agreement between Morris and Gefsky is subject to Morris' obtaining the approval of Screen Actors Guild, Inc. of said SAG Theatrical and Television Motion Picture agency contracts. In the event said approval is not obtained from Screen Actors Guild, Inc. within a period of thirty days (30) from the date of request for same, then this agreement shall be of no force and effect whatsoever, in which event the parties shall retain the same positions each of them had prior to the execution of this agreement and all of the agency contracts executed by Tate, as referred to in Paragraph 1(d) hereof, shall be deemed null and void and Morris shall have no claim against Tate or Gefsky in connection therewith.

4. This agreement sets forth the entire understanding between the parties and may not be cancelled, altered or amended except by an instrument in writing.

IN WITNESS WHEREOF the parties hereto have executed this agreement this _____ day of _____, 1965.

MAR 1 0 1965

WILLIAM MORRIS AGENCY, INC.

By: _____

HAROLD L. GEFSKY AGENCY

By: _____

The undersigned, SHARON TATE, has read the foregoing agreement and understands its terms and conditions. The undersigned hereby consents to the foregoing agreement and approves and agrees to be bound by each and every term and condition of the agreement insofar as they are applicable to her.

_____
SHARON TATE

Mr. Ed TV Show

Sharon appeared in two episodes titled "Ed Discovers America," which aired on October 13, 1963. She appears as the girl in the park. She was also in "Love Thy New Neighbor," which aired on December 15, 1936. She was a telephone operator.

Petticoat Junction TV Show

Also in 1963, Sharon was cast as Billie Jo Bradley in *Petticoat Junction,* but the part never materialized because Martin Ransohoff, her manager, advised her to walk away. He said he felt it was not a good career move.

It was also reported that producers of the show found out about some "skimpy" photos of Sharon and felt it would not work well with the clean-cut image of the show. They cast Jeannine Riley for the role instead. Only publicity photos exist of Sharon posing with the other girls.

The cast that never was: Pat Woodall, Bea Benaderat, Linda Kaye and Sharon.

The Beverly Hillbillies TV Show

In 1963, after *Petticoat Junction* she then went on to do a *Beverly Hillbillies* episode with greater success as he first appeared in the episode "Elly Starts To School," the fourth episode of the second season. She portrayed a student with blonde hair. She made an impression on the producers and would appear in 14 additional episodes as Miss Hathaway's secretary at the Commerce Bank, Janet Trego. This time she wore a black wig. The episodes spanned from 1963–1965.

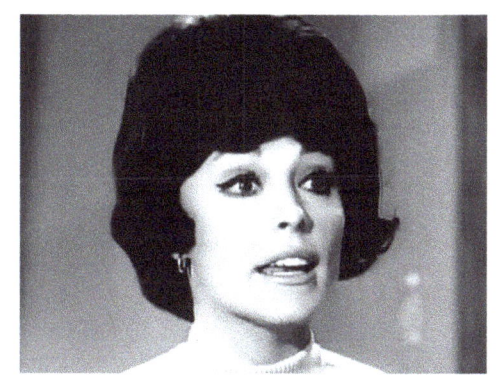

Max Baer

"When I first met Sharon on the set of *The Beverly Hillbillies*, I thought she was the prettiest girl I had ever seen and a knockout beauty. She was terrific," Max Baer, who portrayed Jethro in the series, said on the *Jerry Springer Show* that reunited the cast in the 1980s. Baer said he dated Sharon Tate on a couple of occasions, and she accompanied him to the Emmy Awards.

When I met Max Bear at a Hollywood Collector's Show, I asked him, to inscribe a photo to my wife Mary and me, and also express his feelings for Sharon in a few words. He graciously did just that:

SHARON TATE AND MAX BAER JR.
BEVERLY HILLBILLIES

**Sharon's original signed contract for *The Beverly Hillbillies*
episode titled "The Clampetts Versus Automation" from April 1965**

ACTORS TELEVISION MOTION PICTURE DAY PLAYERS CONTRACT

Company **FILMWAYS TV PRODUCTIONS, INC.** Dated **April 2, 1965**

Date of Employment Starts **April 5, 1965** Name **SHARON TATE**

Part **"JANET TREGO"** Address **9610 Easton Dr., Beverly Hills**

Production Title **"CLAMPETTS VERSUS AUTOMATION"** Telephone No. **OL-2-7011**

Production Number **#5000-102** Social Security No. **452-74-4733**

Daily Rate **$150.00** Legal Resident of What State

Weekly Conversion Rate Citizen of U.S.

Married Quota No.

Date of Birth Date of Entry U.S.

This agreement covers the employment of the above-named Player by _____ in the production and at the rate of compensation set forth above and is subject to and shall include, for the benefit of the Player and the Producer, all of the applicable provisions and conditions contained or provided for in the 1964 Screen Actors Guild Television Agreement (herein called the "Television Agreement"). Player's employment shall include performance in non-commercial openings, closings, bridges, etc., and no added compensation shall be payable to Player so long as such are used in the role and episode covered hereunder in which Player appears; for other use, Player shall be paid the added minimum compensation, if any, required under the provisions of the Screen Actors Guild Agreements with Producer.

Producer shall have all the rights in and to the results and proceeds of the Player's services rendered hereunder, as are provided with respect to "photoplays" in Schedule B of the 1952 SAC Codified Basic Agreement as amended.

Producer shall have the unlimited right throughout the world to telecast the film or exhibit the film theatrically in accordance with the terms and conditions of the Television Agreement.

If the motion picture is rerun on television in the United States or Canada and contains any of the results and proceeds of the Player's services, the Player will be paid for each day of employment hereunder the amounts entered in the blanks in this paragraph, or, if the blanks are not filled in, the Player will be paid the minimum additional compensation prescribed therefor by the Television Agreement.

| 2nd run | 3rd run | 4th run | 5th run | 6th and all succeeding runs |

If there is foreign telecasting of the motion picture as defined in Section 14, of the Television Agreement, and such motion picture contains any of the results and proceeds of the Player's services, the Player will be paid the amount in the blank space below for each day of employment hereunder, or if such blank space is not filled in, then the Player will be paid the minimum additional compensation prescribed therefor by the Television Agreement.

If the motion picture is exhibited theatrically anywhere in the world and contains any of the results and proceeds of the Player's services, the Player will be paid for each day of employment hereunder $_____ or if this blank is not filled in, then the Player will be paid the minimum additional compensation prescribed therefor by the Television Agreement.

The Player (does) (does not) hereby authorize the Producer to deduct from the compensation and advances hereinabove specified an amount equal to 1% of each installment of compensation and advances due the Player hereunder and payable during the employment, and to pay the amount so deducted to the Motion Picture Relief Fund of America, Inc.

Sharon Tate   By *Bill Finn*
Player   Producer

Enterprise Printers and Stationers
7529 Sunset L.A. 46, CALIF. Telephone: 876-3533   24

**Original script for the episode "The Giant Jackrabbit" in 1963
Sharon was cast as Janet Trego**

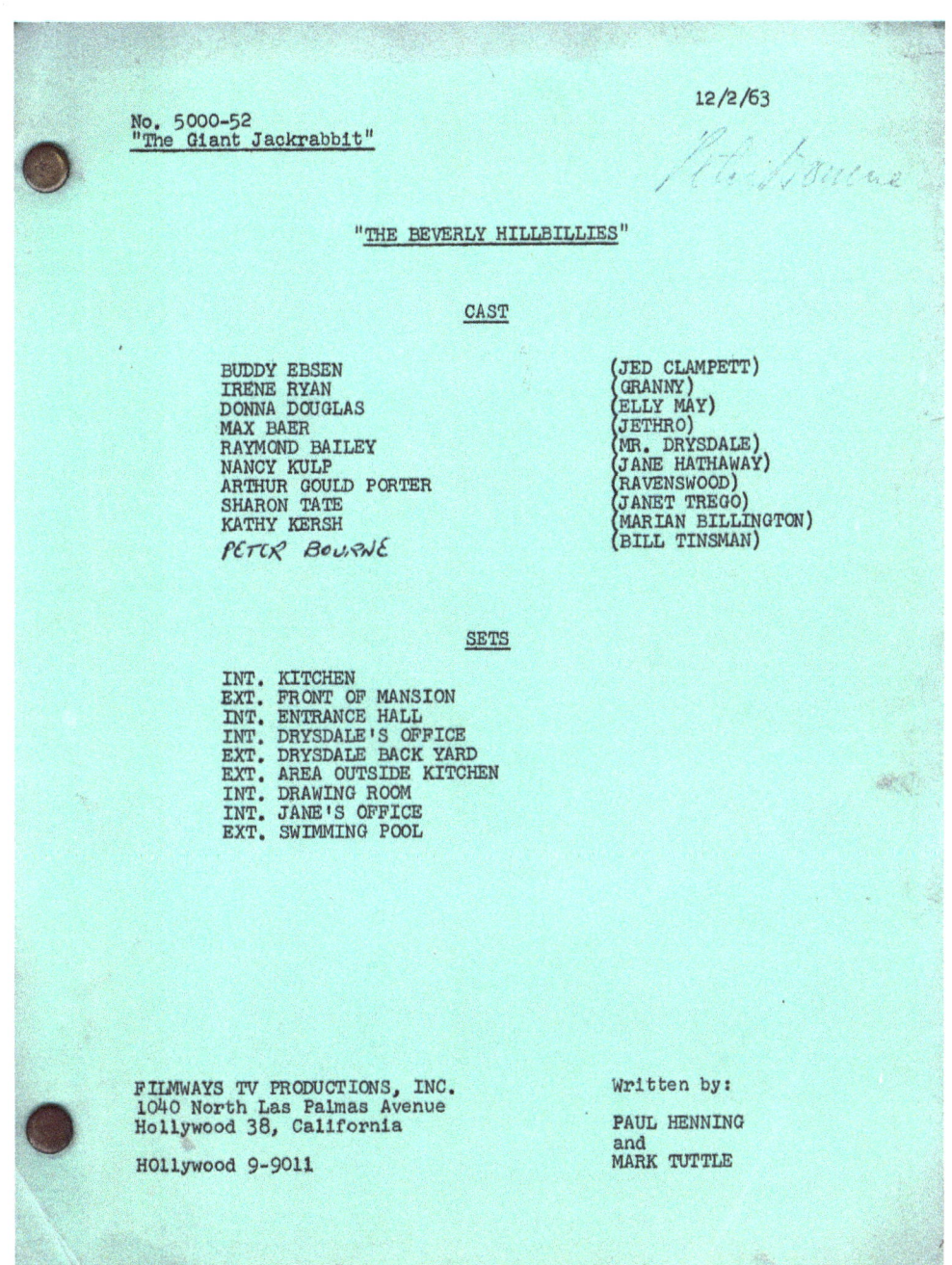

The Man From U.N.C.L.E. TV Show

"The Girls of Nazarone Affair" is the episode of The Man From U.N.C.L.E. that featured Sharon Tate. It aired on Friday, April 12, 1965. It was the second to last episode of the first season and aired in black and white.

In this episode, Napoleon Solo and Illya Kuriyakin, played by Robert Vaughn and David McCallum, arrive in Greece and head to the Athens Riviera. They're searching for a strength-enhancing miracle formula developed by Dr. Kelvin (who you never see), that is missing. U.N.C.L.E. was hired to protect the doctor and the formula, but he's killed before they arrive. There are many twists and turns in the storyline. The two agents are surrounded by Lucia Nazarone, Lavinia, Madame Streigau of THRUSH (the recurring archenemy in the series) and her three blonde assistants, one of which is Sharon Tate who plays the therapist . No matter how many times these women try to kill Napoleon and Illya, the agents are victorious in the end and are ready to move on to their next AFFAIR adventure. The show ran for four seasons, from 1964-1968.

An honorable mention in this episode is the excellent footage of one of the all-time classic cars, the Cobra Roadster in its racing form, something rarely seen in a classic TV show like this. Well done!

I watched *The Man From U.N.C.L.E.* with my family on Friday nights when it first aired in the 1960s, but this episode got past me and I didn't know Sharon appeared in it until long after the show was no longer on the air.

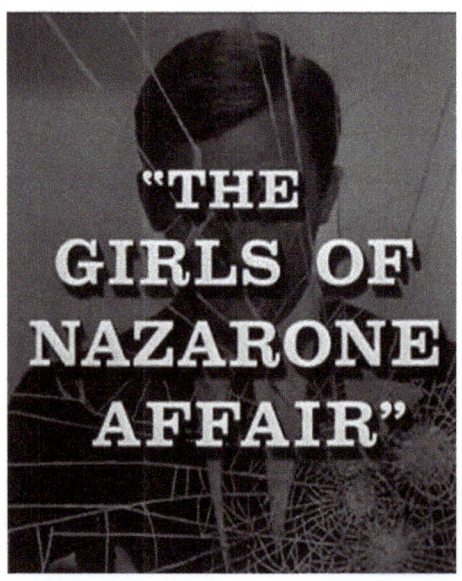

Publicity photos of Sharon and David McCallum from the episode and the paperback titled The Man From U.N.C.L.E. *Notice the story title is different from the episode.*

The Merv Griffin Show

In August 1966 when in London, Sharon Tate took Merv Griffin of *The Merv Griffin Show* on a tour of Carnaby Street and Kings Road, two of London's hottest fashion spots at that time. Tate and Merv walked down the posh streets, with fashion enthusiast Merv asking Sharon anything and everything from high fashion ("Oh, are these mini skirts?") to Carnaby Street's history, and of course, Sharon's blossoming film career.

Strolling past the London crowds, Sharon gracefully answered all of Merv's questions, also explaining the recent origins of the path they were treading, stating, "Carnaby Street started with The Beatles and The Rolling Stones." After that, they proceeded to the end of the street before coming across a group of boys Merv thought were wearing mini skirts. Tate, again corrected her interviewer, saying, "They're not wearing mini-skirts. They're boy scouts," which seemed to amuse Griffin. In impromptu fashion, Merv also ran into actor Hugh O'Brian, who was making a picture there and introduced Sharon to him. Pretty cool.

Next, Merv can be seen taking Sharon's hand and running across to the other cultural hot spot — Kings Road. It was there where they finally got around to their "interview," with Merv then asking her about her film career in Hollywood and the upcoming projects she'd be featured in. Merv mentioned he had heard that Sharon was going to be in "a monster movie soon. No not really, it's called *The Fearless Vampire Killers*. It sounds terrible, but it's a comedy celebrating the satire on horror films. It's kind of like a live Walt Disney film." He then declared the film's director proudly: "It's Roman Polanski!" And the rest as they say is history.

Thanks to YouTube.com, the entire interview can be seen. It is fun experiencing London in the 1960s and how Griffin becomes quite fond of Sharon as the interview progresses.

The Tonight Show Starring Johnny Carson

Sharon Tate made an appearance to promote her upcoming four movies on the *The Tonight Show with Johnny Carson* on August 2, 1967. Unfortunately in the original videotape of the show was reused, so Sharon's appearance was lost.

Playboy After Dark, Hosted by Hugh M. Hefner

This second episode of the syndicated television show was taped on July 24, 1968, and was first aired in Los Angeles on February 7, and then on February 22 in New York in 1969. The premise of the show featured guests from entertainers, movie and television stars, music groups, stand up comedians and members of the Broadway stage, all in a casual atmosphere with Hefner as the host, leading the conversations.

The central figures of the second episode were Sharon Tate and her husband, Roman Polanski, who was just coming off the success of the film he directed titled *Rosemary's Baby*. Hefner asked Sharon about nudity in movies and she politely answered, "If the part is as natural as making love and taking a bath, etc. it's fine, but if it is contrived it becomes vulgar." This was Sharon's last television appearance, as she was heading to Italy to do the film *12+1* aka *The 13 Chairs*.

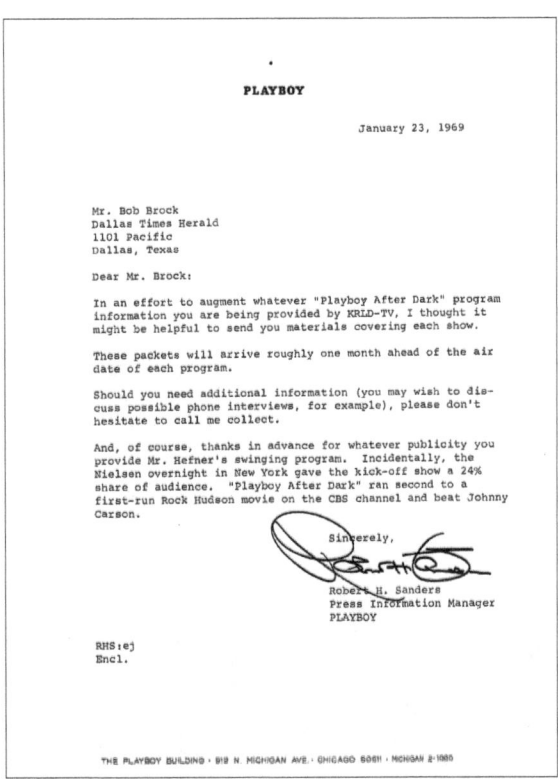
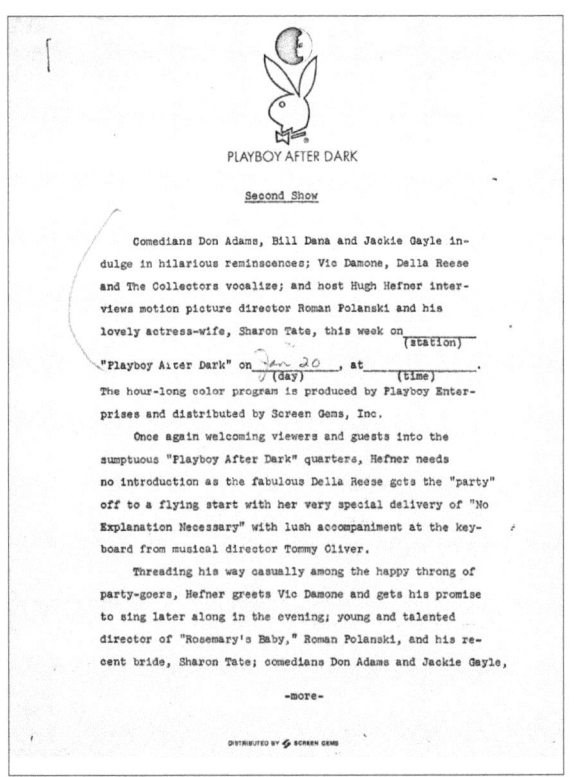

Hugh Hefner's promotional pitch for *Playboy After Dark* (from the original release shown below)

When the announcement was made that we were about to start production on "Playboy After Dark," there was an immediate assumption on the part of many people that the nation's living rooms would soon be invaded by an electronic version of Playboy with particular emphasis upon the pretty girls long identified with the magazine.

Quite obviously, TV is not ready for a literal exposition of Playboy's contents, although it does seem to me that TV is becoming increasingly mature.

Television's considerable headway in presenting more sophisticated programming is an accomplishment achieved in spite of the super-sensitivities of the electronic medium which all too often seems to run a rather frightened race.

The viewer's receptivity to a greater degree of sophistication is no doubt one of the more apparent manifestations of the sweeping social changes that have taken place in this country. Many of these changes, I might add, have attracted a great deal of Playboy's editorial attention.

Television's climate of greater sophistication, particularly in appropriate time segments, is one of the major reasons why we chose to create "Playboy After Dark." The very substantial success of programs such as Rowan and Martin's "Laugh-In" and "The Smothers Brothers" added greatly in the timing of our decision. The deftly directed irreverence of these shows offers splendid proof that the viewing public is simply tired of the seemingly endless parade of banalities which constitute far too much of TV's total product.

The nation's healthy maturation is further provable when you consider that Jack Parr's famous water closet incident, in which the humorist was virtually banned from his network program, occurred less than ten years ago. Since that time, the list of taboo subjects has been reduced rather realistically by the ever more adult offerings of programs hosted by such personalities as John Carson and Merv Griffin.

While the Carson and Griffin shows inevitably wind up with four people on a couch engaging in conversation with the host, "Playboy After Dark" has the kind of flexibility afforded by a party format. As a guest at our parties, the viewer feels an unusual degree of involvement.

We think you will find "Playboy After Dark" provocative, entertaining and a highly contemporary program.

* * *

*"I'd like to be an American Catherine Deneuve.
She plays beautiful, sensitive, deep parts
with a little bit of intelligence behind them."*

– Sharon Tate

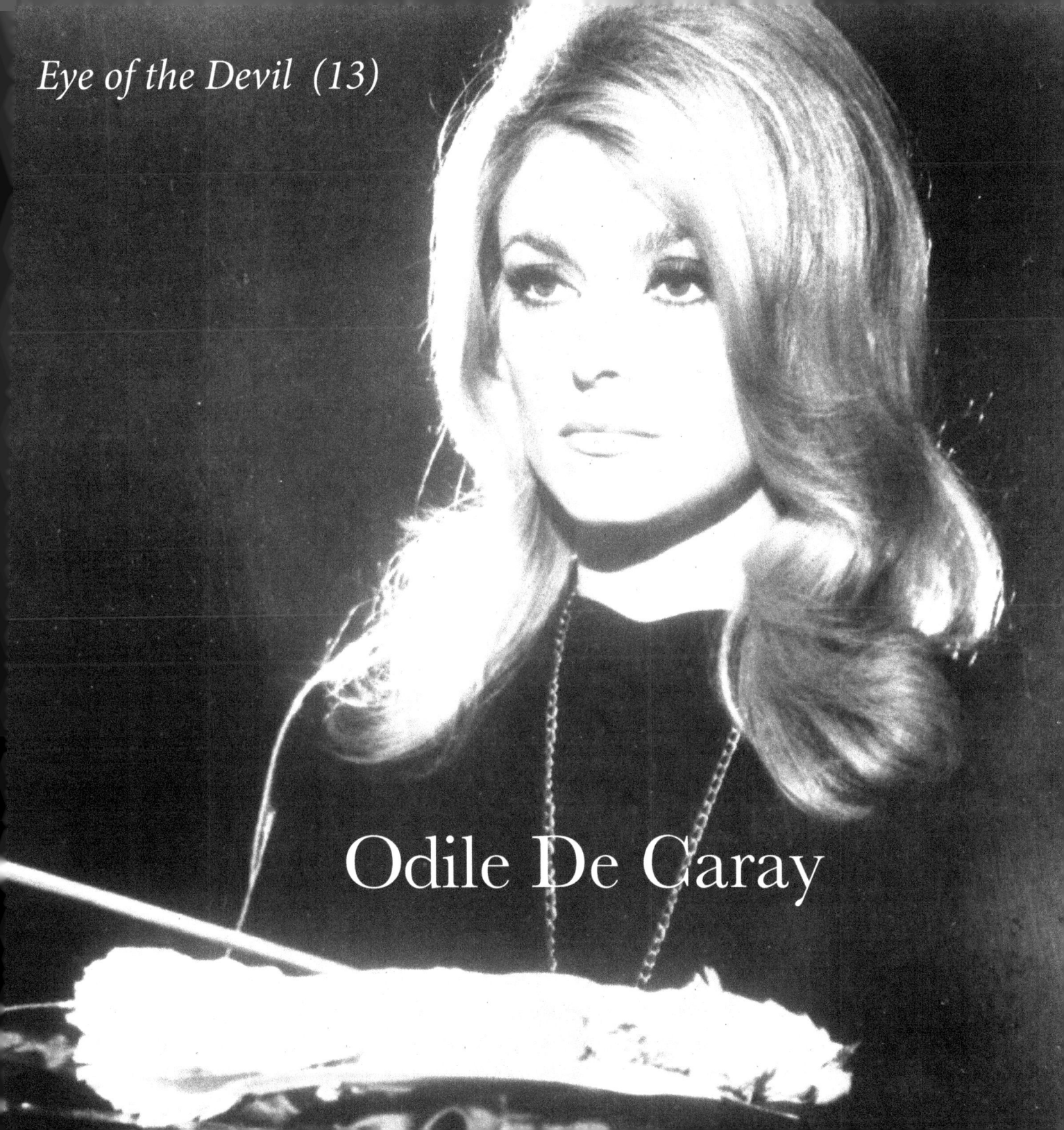

Eye of the Devil (13)

Odile De Caray

"I discovered regardless of how many months and years of acting classes that I have had, I found that I know absolutely nothing at all. So now I can begin"

– Sharon Tate

Quote from *All Eyes on Sharon Tate* featurette

All Eyes on Sharon Tate (Promotional Featurette)

This was the behind the scenes short promo film showcasing the cinema's newest star at MGM, Sharon Tate. Filmed in England, the featurette takes a look at Sharon at play, as well as dancing with *Eye of the Devil* co-star David Hemmings at a discotheque, romping with the pigeons at Hyde park, and then follows her to her acting and speech class for her part in the upcoming film *Eye of the Devil,* also starring David Niven. Niven speaks quite fondly of the 22 year old and the bright future ahead of her in films. The film also stars Deborah Kerr.

Next, she is rehearsing scenes for the film and highlights a modeling session that would to eventually grace the cover of *Photoplay* magazine at the conclusion. It is a great insight for the up and coming young talent hence the title...

All Eyes on Sharon Tate.

Eye of the Devil (13)

Filming from: September–December 1965

First released November 18, 1966 in Italy • US release (New York) December 6, 1967 • London from MGM on March 7

Sharon's character: Odile de Caray

Eye of the Devil, initially titled *13*, is a British black and white horror film set in rural France. It was filmed at the Chateau de Hautefort and at MGM British Studios in Borehamwood, England. The cast of the movie consisted of: David Niven, Kim Novak, David Hemmings, Donald Pleasance and introduced Sharon Tate. The film was directed by J. Lee Thompson. Novak injured her back in a riding accident in November with only two weeks of filming left to complete. This shut the film down until they found a replacement — enter Deborah Kerr. As a result many scenes had to be re-shot and filming resumed in December.

The film tells the story of the family of Marquis Philippe de Montfaucon (David Niven), which has long been the major landowner in Bellenac, a wine growing region in France. Philippe receives word that there are problems in the fields that threaten this year's harvest, so he leaves his wife and children at their home in Paris and sets out for Bellenac.

Against her husband's wishes, Marquise Catherine de Montfaucon (Deborah Kerr) decides to follow Philippe back to Bellenac, taking their two adolescent children, Jacques (Robert Duncan) and Antoinette (Suky Appleby), along with her. Once there, Catherine sees disturbing behavior involving two young adult siblings who are hanging around the estate, Christian (David Hemmings) and Odile de Caray (Sharon Tate). She finds out the two are from a family that has also lived in the region for generations. Catherine witnesses Christian killing a dove with a bow and arrow, and Odile seems to have a hypnotic power over anyone within her sight.

Catherine also observes that Philippe seems to be in a trance while in Bellenac. Christian and Odile threaten Catherine and her children in an attempt to make them leave, but she decides to stay so she can figure out what is happening and possibly save Philippe, because she believes he's in danger.

When Catherine eventually learns what is going on, it may be too late to save Philippe, and perhaps Jacques, from their evil destiny. The fate of the men of the de Montfaucon family in Bellenac is never good because the old pagan rituals they follow call for the life of the Marquis to save the crops.

Eye of the Devil premiered in New York on December 6, 1967. *The New York Times* reviews referred to Tate's performance on screen as "chillingly beautiful but expressionless," and if you watch the movie that is the way she was suppose to portray Odile.

Although she was American, England claimed Sharon Tate as their own in various magazines and newspapers. Sharon was asked what it was like to act with such a distinguished cast in her premiere performance, and she answered: *"Of course I was nervous but I was flattered rather than intimidated because everybody put me at such ease. They are such pros. You don't see their technique but when you are surrounded by the best."*

Cast Member-Signed from *Eye of the Devil*

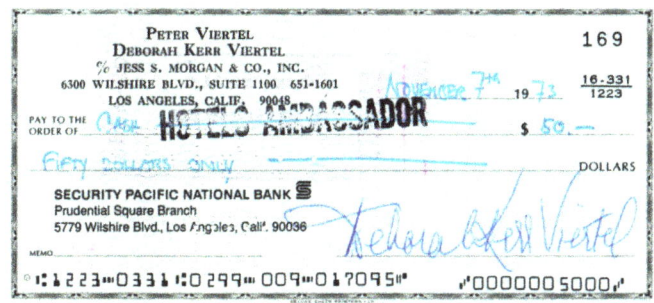

David Niven - Philippe De Montfaucon

Sharon Tate - Odile de Caray

Deborah Kerr - Catherine de Montfaucon

David Hemmings - Christian de Caray

Promotional - Press - Publication Material for *Eye of the Devil*

Eye of the Devil *promotional radio spot announcements from MGM.*

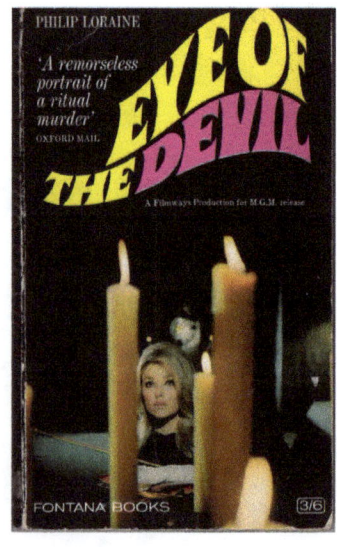

Original synopsis and cast biography booklet for *Eye of the Devil*

CAST
OF
"EYE OF THE DEVIL"

RUNNING TIME 92 MIN.
September 7 RELEASE
TRADE REVIEW DATE
September 7th

```
CATHERINE . . . . . . . . . . . . . . . DEBORAH KERR
PHILIPPE DE MONTFAUCON . . . . . . . DAVID NIVEN
PERE DOMINIC . . . . . . . . . . . . DONALD PLEASENCE
JEAN-CLAUDE IBERT . . . . . . . . . . EDWARD MULHARE
COUNTESS ESTELLE . . . . . . . . . . FLORA ROBSON
ALAIN DE MONTFAUCON . . . . . . . . EMLYN WILLIAMS
ODILE . . . . . . . . . . . . . . . . . . SHARON TATE
CHRISTIAN DE CARAY . . . . . . . . . DAVID HEMMINGS
DR. MONNET . . . . . . . . . . . . . JOHN LE MESURIER
ANTOINETTE . . . . . . . . . . . . . SUKY APPLEBY
RENNARD . . . . . . . . . . . . . . DONALD BISSET
JACQUES . . . . . . . . . . . . . . ROBERT DUNCAN
GRANDEC . . . . . . . . . . . . . . MICHAEL MILLER
```

Produced by
JOHN CALLEY and MARTIN RANSOHOFF

Directed by
J. LEE THOMPSON

Screenplay by
ROBIN ESTRIDGE and DENNIS MURPHY

Based on the novel "Day of the Arrow" by
PHILIP LORAINE

Director of Photography
ERWIN HILLIER, B.S.C.

Music by
GARRY McFARLAND

Main Titles Designed by.........Maurice Binder
Costumes by.....................Julie Harris

MARTIN RANSOHOFF'S PRODUCTION
A Filmways Picture
Presented by
METRO-GOLDWYN-MAYER

-6-22-67-

Movie posters and lobby cards for *Eye of the Devil (13)*

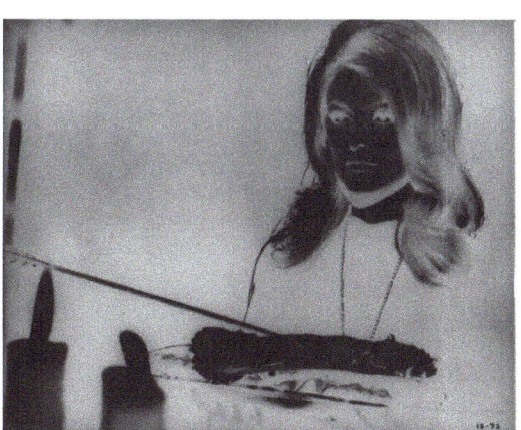

Lobby stills and original 8 x10 negatives for the production of the movie.

I'm very unpredictable.

Very, very impulsive. Extremely. Absolutely!

Sometimes I don't know what I want to do from one day to the next.

I can't enjoy anything premeditated;

I just do it as I feel it.

But whatever I do is motivated by honesty.

– Sharon Tate

*"Roman is a fascinating, creative director.
When I first met him, it was a case of instant hate.
He was so blunt. But now it's all music."
– Sharon Tate*

The Fearless Vampire Killers or *Pardon Me but Your Teeth are in My Neck*

Filming from April–June 1966 • US release date: November 13, 1967 from MGM
Sharon's Character: Sarah Shagal

The Fearless Vampire Killers, originally released in the UK as *Dance of the Vampires,* is a horror/comedy film directed by Roman Polanski, who also co-wrote the film. It co-starred Polanski's future wife, Sharon Tate. They met and fell in love while filming the movie. Sharon, as Sarah Shagal, was absolutely beautiful on screen, and even with very little dialogue made her presence known.

The film is set "deep in the heart of Transylvania" and the story takes place some time during the mid-19th century. Polanski stars as Alfred, one of two hunters entering a small village at the end of a long search for signs of vampires. The two stay at a local inn full of angst-ridden townspeople who perform strange rituals to fend off an unseen evil. This is where Alfred develops a crush for Sarah, the over-protected daughter of the tavern keeper. Alfred later witnesses Sarah being kidnapped by the local vampire lord, Count von Krolock (played by Ferdy Maine, who also narrates the film).

The highlight of the film is the dance finale, filled with colorful costumes from the era. Sharon looks beautiful with her long locks of red hair, and is quite entertaining as well. As you watch, you think that Alfred saves his fair maiden Sarah from the vampires during the dance, since he takes her to a waiting sled, manned by his fellow hunter (Professor Abronsius, played by Jack MacGowren). It seems as though they sled away and live happily ever after. Guess again!

This was Polanski's first feature film to be photographed in color using a widescreen 2.35:1 aspect ratio which was innovative at the time..

The Fearless Vampire Killers was first released in the United States by MGM on November 13, 1967. Roman and Sharon attended the premiere of the movie in Paris on January 31,1968, the movie was finally released in the UK in December 1968. A week earlier Roman had to defend Sharon when she was accosted in the streets of Paris while they were still on their honeymoon and at the Premiere, Roman still had his bandage on his face from the incident.

Playboy *magazine from March 1967, featuring a nude pictorial layout of Sharon on the set of The Fearless Vampire Killers.*

Original (first draft) script for *The Vampire Killers* — the working title — dated January 17, 1966

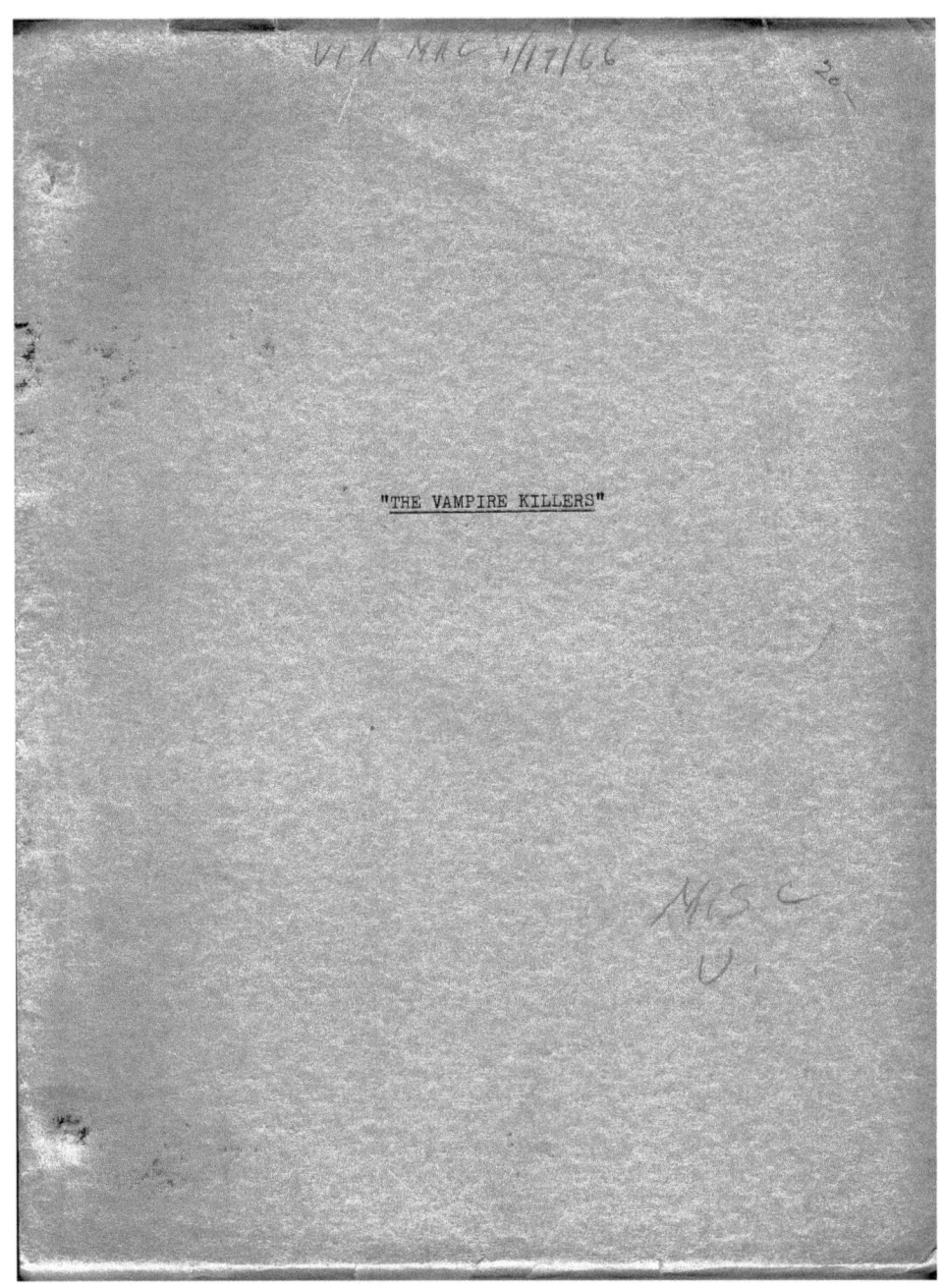

Promotional materials for *The Fearless Vampire Killers*

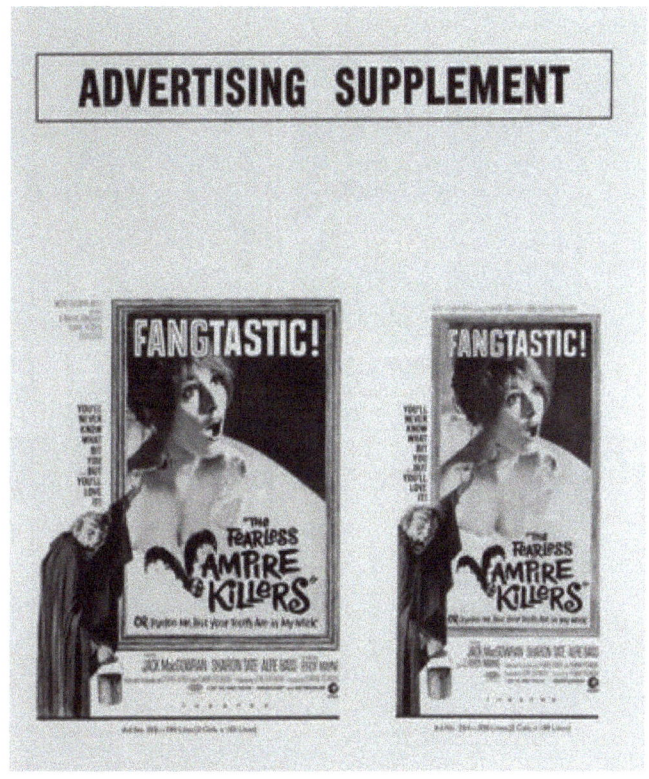

Original advertising artwork plate with promotional print supplement

Movie posters and lobby cards (domestic and foreign) for *The Fearless Vampire Killers*

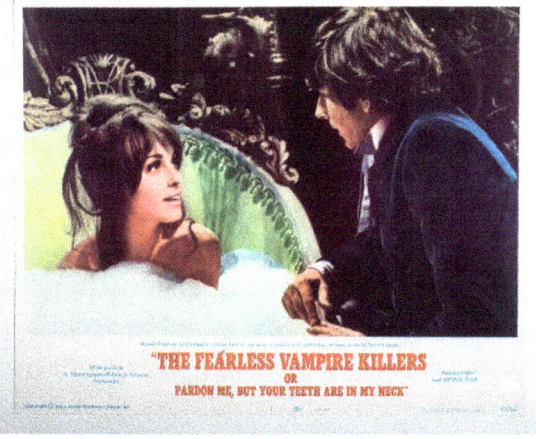

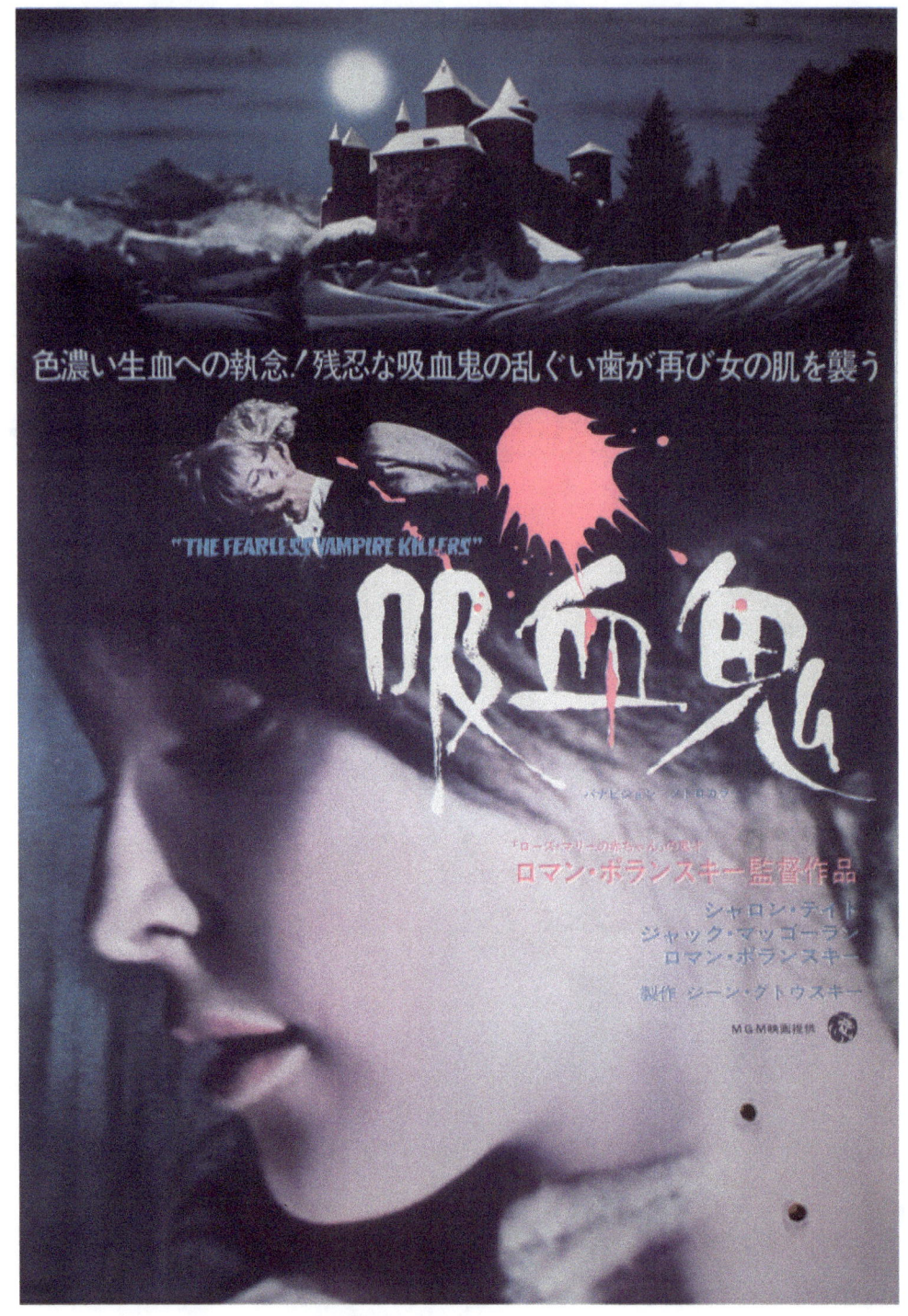

Sharon Tate's autograph.

Roman Polanski autographed lobby still.

The Fearless Vampire Killers *Deluxe Letter Box Edition (long out of print) laser disc on MGM Home Video was released in 1993, featuring Director Roman Polanski's uncut and uncensored international version, which is 20 minutes longer than the original American release. There were extras complimenting the incredible cover artwork, including the theatrical trailer from 1967, alternate main title sequence, and the 11 minute featurette,* All Eyes on Sharon Tate *highlighted in the Odele de Caray* (Eye of the Devil) *chapter.*

"My definition of love is being full.
Complete.
It makes everything lighter.
Beauty is something you see.
Love is something you feel."

– Sharon Tate

Jay & Roman

"I'm one of those mad, irrational characters who simply loves men.
I love them because they're men.
Women, …I don't like to compete against them or play games.
It's a waste of time."
– Sharon Tate

The Jay Sebring and Roman Polanski Connection
(The Men in Sharon's Life)

Jay Sebring (aka Thomas John Kummer) was known as the hairstylist to the stars. He was born on October 10, 1933 and grew up in Detroit, Michigan with his two sisters and brother. After graduating high school in 1951, Jay went into the Navy and fought for his country for 4 years in the Korean War. After the war, Jay found time for a personal life and married model Bonnie Lee Marple in 1960. The Marriage only lasted three years, ending in 1963.

Jay attended and graduated from beauty school and opened his first a shop on Fairfax and Melrose in Los Angeles. He promptly invented a whole new way of cutting men's hair. His innovations including shampooing men's hair before styling it, cutting with scissors instead of clippers, and using blow dryers was new to the United States. He even created and branded his own hairspray for men.

His big break came after meeting actress Barbara Luna at a party. She told singer Vic Damone, who liked him enough to fly him to Las Vegas to cut his hair. Vic then introduced Sebring, still known as Thomas Kummer, to Rat Pack members Frank Sinatra and Peter Lawford who later continued to have Jay style their hair. Thomas Kummer then renamed himself after the Sebring International Raceway, after seeing a pictorial magazine layout of the track.

His other star-studded clients included Steve McQueen, Warren Beatty, Henry Fonda, Kirk Douglas and Jim Morrison from The Doors. Sebring even assisted in launching the film career of martial artist and actor Bruce Lee. After meeting Lee at the Long Beach International Karate Championships in 1964, he introduced Lee to his producer friend William Dozier, who started Lee's career with *The Green Hornet*.

Due to his popularity in Hollywood and being friends with Dozier, Jay made a brief appearance on one of the most popular TV shows at the time, *Batman*. His character was Mr. Oceanspring, who was also a hairstylist. Pretty cool!

He made a few more TV appearances, including a part on the *Virginian* as a barber, and in early 1963 he appeared on a episode of *To Tell The Truth* as himself.

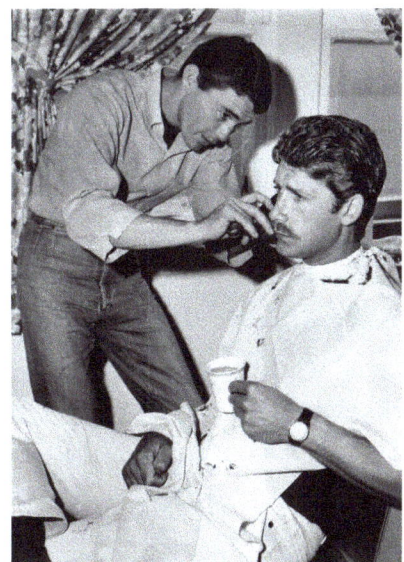

It all changed for Jay in October of 1964 when he was first introduced to Sharon Tate by journalist Joe Hyams. They immediately hit it off and began a romantic relationship, and later a very close friendship. They spent a lot of time together up until she left for London to act in her first film, *Eye of the Devil* in 1965.

While Sharon was away, she even prepared a letter to the William Morris Agency stating that when she would be out of out of the country, and asking that any compensation she would receive be sent to Jay. That is how close they were. Eventually, Jay would go to London and to be with Sharon but would leave before filming was complete.

Sharon got back to London in early 1966 to work on her next film, *The Fearless Vampire Killers*, where she met the director of the movie and co-star, Roman Polanski. Sparks flew for immediately for Roman and Sharon.

They became close during the filming. Roman took semi-nude but very tasteful and playful shots of her on a set break, as she felt comfortable around him.

Roman was born Raymond Thierry Liebling on August 18, 1933, which is coincidently the same year Jay Sebring was born. Roman had many accomplishments over the years, including director, producer, screenwriter, and actor. His Polish/Jewish parents moved from Paris, his birthplace, back to Poland in 1937 and two years later Poland was invaded by Nazi Germany. World War II caused the family to suffer greatly as they were trapped there. Sadly, his parents were taken in raids, which left Roman in foster homes with a new identity, but he survived the Holocaust.

When he first started making films in 1962, he was already known for his foreign films and was honored with an Academy Award nomination for best Foreign Language Film for *Knife in the Water*, which was made in Poland. He directed many films and was touted as one of the best directors in cinema. Films included *Repulsion* in 1965 and in the United States he directed what would be his most famous films to date starring Mia Farrow and John Cassevettes, the horror film *Rosemary's Baby* in 1968.

Sharon's romance with Jay ended when she and Roman began a serious relationship. Jay was totally devoted to Sharon and wanted her to be happy, so he traveled to London to meet Polanski and ended up befriending him. They stayed close to him and Sharon.

Roman commented later: "Despite Sebring's lifestyle, he was a very lonely person who regarded Sharon and I as his family."

By this time, Sharon and Roman were the hot Hollywood/London couple being seen everywhere, including movie premiers, award shows, concerts and on vacation with friends.

Sharon on the set of Rosemary's Baby.

Sharon and Roman married on January 20, 1968 in Chelsea, London. Sharon's co-star from *Valley of The Dolls*, Barbara Parkins, was her maid of honor. They shared an incredible flat in London and had friends over for parties before heading back to the states in 1969. Jay was busy as well. In 1967, he opened the company Sebring International to franchise his salons and sell hair care products. In the summer of 1968, Roman and Sharon introduced him to Polanski's friend Wojciech Frykowski and his girlfriend, Folgers coffee heiress Abigail Folger, who had recently moved to Los Angeles from the east coast. They later invested in Sebring's hair care products for men.

Original negative of Sharon on her wedding day, January 20, 1968.

In early May 1969, Sebring opened a new salon at 629 Commercial Street in San Francisco and had a reception on the salon's behalf, attended by several guests, clients and Hollywood royalty. During the summer, Jay would often visit Sharon and Roman's home on Cielo Drive or she would visit Jay at his home.

He even kept a very pregnant Sharon company and took care of her while Roman was overseas doing a movie. He stayed devoted to Sharon until the day of his untimely passing in August 1969.

Sharon and Roman candid pictures on holiday

Jay's Gift to Sharon

Roman's Gift to Sharon

KENT WARNER

To Whom It May Concern:

This letter will be included with the sale of a large round gold compact that belonged to my close friend Sharon Tate. This compact has an inscription, which reads, " Sharon, All My Love... Roman",

It was a gift to Sharon by Roman Polanski who later became her husband, he gave this item to her as a gift after the filming wrapped on the movie, "Fearless Vampire Killers", in which they met and fell in love.

Sharon often stayed at my house and often left behind her personal belongings, this is how I acquired this item. I never got the chance to give her back this compact, or the rest of her things, for she was tragically murdered in August of 1969.

I Certify that all of the above is correct.

Sincerely,

Kent Warner

"Sexiness is all in the eye of the beholder.

I think it should be.

Absolutely.

My sex appeal, whatever it might be, isn't obvious . . .

at least to me.

– Sharon Tate

Don't Make Waves
Filming from August–September 1966 • US release date June 20, 1967 from MGM
Sharon's Character: Malibu

Don't Make Waves is a light-hearted American beach romp with sexual overtones, distributed by MGM. It starred Tony Curtis, Claudia Cardinale and Sharon Tate. The film was Sharon's third produced movie but was the first to be released in cinemas, so it is generally considered to be her debut. Sharon played Malibu, a gorgeous surfer and skydiver who rescues Tony Curtis's character, Carlo Cofield. His attraction for her begins then, even though Malibu has a body builder boyfriend, portrayed by Dave Draper. Through constant manipulation, Carlo pursues romance with Malibu but once he captures her heart, he finds out they have nothing in common. The film takes a dramatic turn when a mudslide caused by a sudden storm makes Carlo's house slide down a cliff. After the characters do some soul searching, and everyone is saved, Malibu goes back to Draper and Tony pairs off with Laura (Cardinele).

MGM mounted an extensive publicity campaign upon the film's release that was based largely on Sharon and her character, Malibu. Life-sized cardboard cutouts of Tate wearing a bikini were placed in cinema foyers throughout the US. It was also linked to a widespread advertising campaign by Coppertone which also featured Sharon. Sharon also attended the *Don't Make Waves* premiere on June 9, 1967, screened during the Sun Fun Festival in Myrtle Beach, South Carolina.

Sharon later told her husband Roman Polanski her experience working on this film was not particularly enjoyable as the production atmosphere was tense, and it was worsened when an stunt man drowned when he parachuted into the Pacific Ocean.

Original and rare one-of-a-kind Polaroid photo taken of Sharon on the beach in August 1966, during the Coppertone ad photo session.

**Original script for *Don't Make Waves*
inscribed on the cover to me and signed by co-star of the film, Tony Curtis**

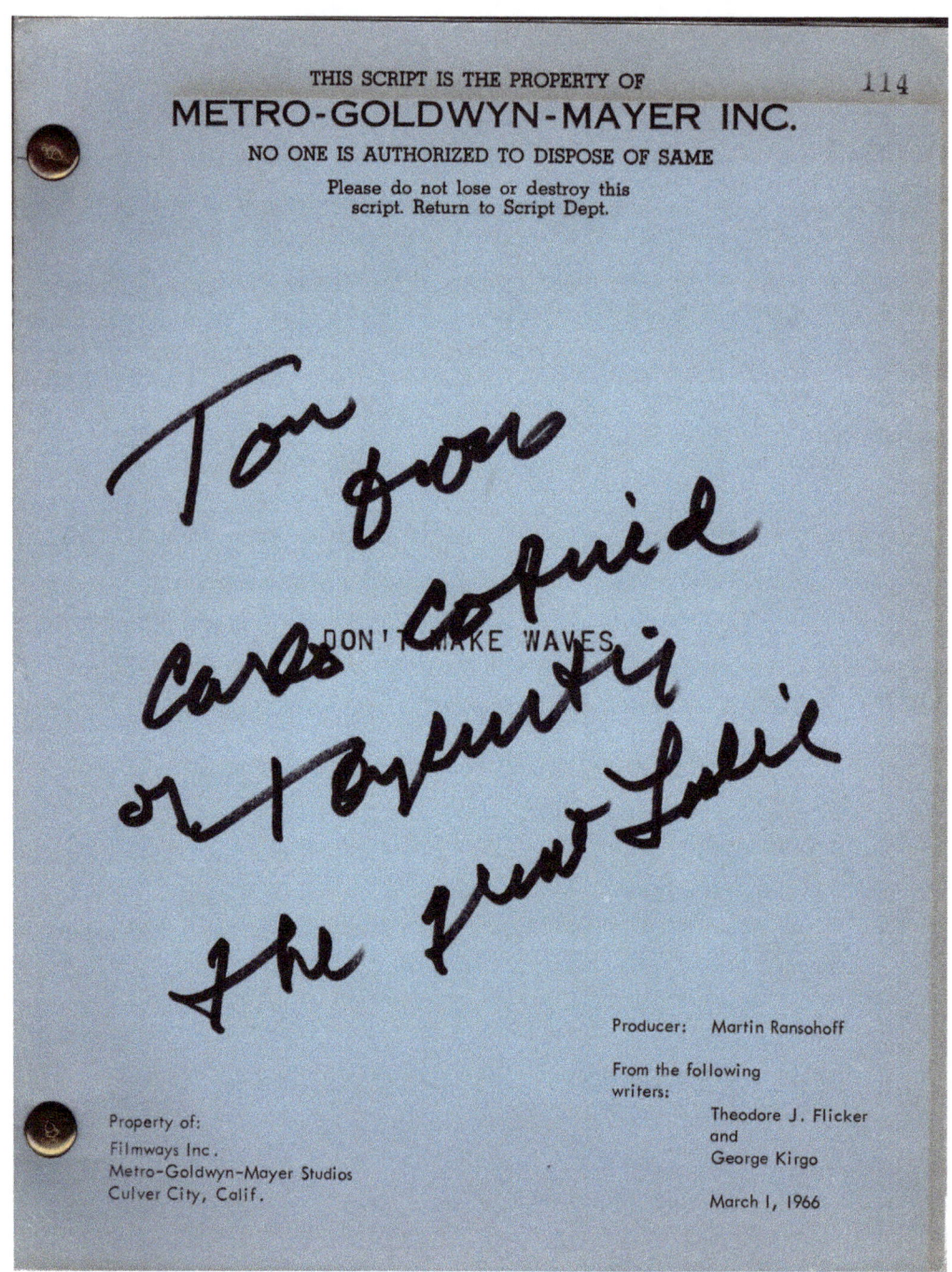

Original Print Advertisement, Soundtrack Album and Tape, Promo Record and US Sheet Music for *Don't Make Waves*

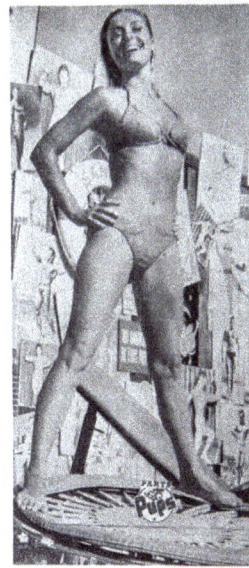

Don't Make Waves
*Promotional Radio Spot
Announcements from MGM*

Original movie posters and program (US and foreign) for *Don't Make Waves*

Don't Make Waves
Danish Movie Program

Don't Make Waves Movie Window Card showing at the Casino Theatre in Hampton Beach, New Hampshire in 1967

US half Sheet Movie poster

Sometimes, I think it would be better to be a sex symbol, because at least I would know where I was... But I'd lose my mind!

– Sharon Tate

Fashion
(Sharon's Personally Owned)

*"I'd like to be a fairy princess –
a little golden doll with gossamer wings,
in a voile dress, adorned with bright, shiny things.
I see that as something totally pure and beautiful."*

– Sharon Tate

As quoted in *Eye* magazine Vol. 2 No. 1 (January 1969)

Roman Polanski

October 7, 1996

To Whom It May Concern:

This letter will show proof that I once gave to my late wife Sharon Tate, this beautiful Pucci pink dress.

This was one of her personal belongings left behind in our home on Cielo Drive when she passed in 1969, that I did not give to her family because of sentimental reasons.

I have decided to donate this item to a Charity for violence against women. I attest to the truth in all of the above.

Sincerely,

Roman

Patricia Hayes
20 west hill road
London
Sw18 England

To Whom It may Concern:

I'm writing this letter as Provenance for a pink colored Emilio Pucci Mini-Dress that I bought when in France, at a charity fundraiser that once belonged to the late actress Sharon Tate.

The item in question was donated by her husband director Roman Polanski. The fundraiser was for "Violence Against Woman" held in Paris in the winter of 1997.

I attest to the truth in the above statement.

Sincerely,

Patricia Hayes

Witnessed by

Bart Friedman

Ben Nye Make-Up Artist Film & TV

2-10-79

To Whom it May Concern,

I worked in the Entertainment industry for many years at many studios as a make-up Artist. During this time I became good friends with many celebrities.

While working on the 1967 film "Valley of the Dolls," I became friendly with this very sweet girl named Sharon Tate. I instantly liked her and we hit it off right away.

Sharon knowing that I collected items from all of the stars I worked with gave me this brown & white lace middle mini-dress with white hoops holding the two pieces together. She wore it to the set one day and left in wardrobe to go to a premier.

I attest that everything stated is 100% percent the truth.

Sincerly,
Ben Nye 2-10-79

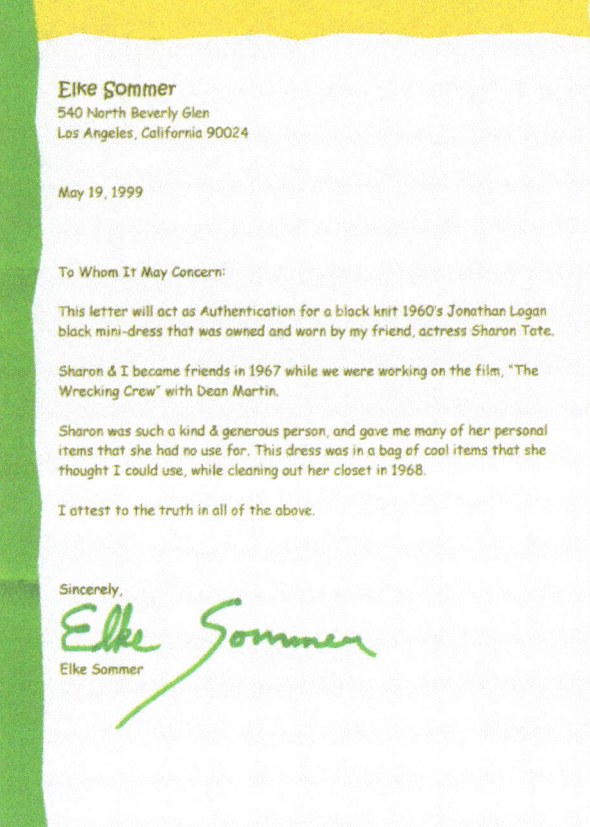

Elke Sommer
540 North Beverly Glen
Los Angeles, California 90024

May 19, 1999

To Whom It May Concern:

This letter will act as Authentication for a black knit 1960's Jonathan Logan black mini-dress that was owned and worn by my friend, actress Sharon Tate.

Sharon & I became friends in 1967 while we were working on the film, "The Wrecking Crew" with Dean Martin.

Sharon was such a kind & generous person, and gave me many of her personal items that she had no use for. This dress was in a bag of cool items that she thought I could use, while cleaning out her closet in 1968.

I attest to the truth in all of the above.

Sincerely,

Elke Sommer
Elke Sommer

Elke Sommer
540 North Beverly Glen
Los Angeles, California
90024

September 17, 1994

To Whom It May Concern:

My name is Elke Sommer and I've been an actress all over the world for many years. In the 1960's I became friends with a fellow actress named Sharon Tate.

Sharon and I became very good friends during the filming of a movie that we both starred in called, "The Wrecking Crew". Sharon was a very sweet impressionable woman who was very easy to be around and very fun.

Sharon gave me this beautiful 1960's patterned greenish brown & white long overcoat, in a bag of clothes that she thought I could make good use of.

I never wore this coat because it didn't feel right to do so after Sharon's Tragic Death in 1969. I've held on to it for many years but have decided that one of Sharon's fans should have it.

I swear that all of the above information is true and that this really was Sharon Tate's overcoat.

Sincerely,

Elke Sommer

Juanita Widner 9/17/94
Witness & Notary

HAL KING

To Whom It May Concern:

This letter will act as a Certificate of Authenticity for a Greenish-brown & white design 1960's overcoat w/ gold buttons that was owned and used by Actress Sharon Tate.

I purchased this & many other items from Actress Elke Sommer who was friends with Sharon, at a Private collectors sale held at the home of Celebrity Collector Jane Withers in 1994.

I attest to all of the above.

Sincerely,
Hal King

Sharon's hat that accompanied the overcoat from the collection of Elke Sommer.

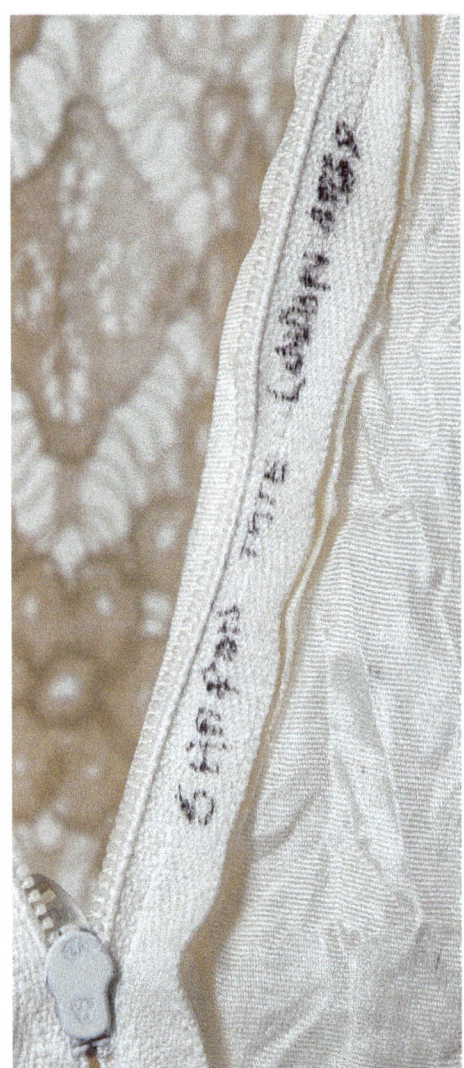

May 16, 1979:

To Whom It May Concern:

My name is Kent Warner. For many years in Hollywood I have worked as a Costumer & Wardrobe Man.

During this time I met and became close friends with Actress Sharon Tate. Sharon was a Lovely girl and knew that i collected personal items from all of my famous friends.

Sharon Herself gave me this lovely eyelet lace mini dress with a scoop neck trimmed with lace sleeve less design from her personal wardrobe. Sharon told me she wore it in London in 1968, so it is noted on the zipper.

I swear to the truth in all that I have stated here and that this dress was owned and worn by Sharon Tate.

Sincerely,

Kent Warner 5/16/1979
Kent Warner
5/16/1979

Margaret R. Headley 5-16-1979
Notary Public 5/16/1979

Edith Lindon

August 18, 1978

To Whom It May Concern:

I worked in Hollywood for a very short time as a make-up and hairstylist.

One of the great opportunities that arose for me was to be the make-up supervisor on the 1967 film,"Valley of the Dolls". During my work on the film, I became very friendly with one of it's stars, the very beautiful, Sharon Tate.

When the film was done shooting, Sharon gave me these white & gold triangle shaped earrings as a memento, to remember her by. Sharon took them off her ears, right in front of me and said, "Edith, I want you to have these". Sharon was a very kind and giving person.

I swear that all of the above is true.

Sincerely,

Edith Lindon
Edith Lindon

Elke Sommer
540 North Beverly Glen
Los Angeles, California
90024

September 17, 1994

To Whom It May Concern:

My name is Elke Sommer and I've been an actress all over the world for many years. In the 1960's I became friends with a fellow actress named Sharon Tate.

Sharon and I became very good friends during the filming of a movie that we both starred in called, "The Wrecking Crew". Sharon was a very sweet impressionable woman who was very easy to be around and very fun.

Sharon gave me this beautiful Chain mesh three angle design necklace, in a bag of clothes that she thought I could make good use of.

I never wore this necklace because it didn't feel right to do so after Sharon's Tragic Death in 1969. I've held on to it for many years but have decided that one of Sharon's fans should have it.

I swear that all of the above information is true and that this really was Sharon Tate's Costume Mesh Necklace.

Sincerely,

Elke Sommer

Elke Sommer

Juanita Widner 9/17/94
Juanita Widner
Witness & Notary

5-12-20

To whom it may concern,
These earrings were once used and worn by Sharon Tate. They were obtained by my uncle who worked in Hollywood for over 40 yrs. at many of the major movie and TV studios. He would often collect disregarded or no longer used items after production was finished or when items were replaced and no longer used... this was one such item. When my uncle died I recieved many of his things from his days in Hollywood which I will slowly sell or auction off. This item was found among his things along with a note describing its origin. I'm sure it will make a nice addition to your collection.

Sincerely,
Ken Ross

Sharon Tate's earrings
Columbia Wardrobe Dept
1968

"It's just as difficult to be pretty as it is to be homely.

People take you from the surface level,

but they'll see an unattractive girl and think

she must have something else."

– Sharon Tate

*"I don't think the movie (Valley of the Dolls) is all that bad.
It's a typical, fantastic, money-making Hollywood picture.
I knew that when I took the part. …
I'm glad I made the movie, but now I need a change."*

– Sharon Tate

Valley of the Dolls

Filming from: March – June 1967 • US release date: December 15, 1967 from 20th Century Fox
Sharon's Character: Jennifer North

Valley of the Dolls is an American drama film based on the 1966 novel of the same name by Jacqueline Susann and was directed by Mark Robson. It is a story of three young women with completely different personalities embarking on their careers. Even though different, they become friends in the city of New York sharing a bond for ambition and falling in and out of romantic relationships. Once fame comes knocking on their door, all three women's lives become more complicated. That eventually leads to drugs (dolls) and alcohol, resulting in tragedy, despair and ultimately strength. Each character's story has a different ending, paralleled by their friendships.

The movie stars Barbara Parkins, who is also known for playing Betty Anderson in the TV show *Peyton Place.* Parkins plays Anne Welles, an innocent but well-educated girl who comes to new York and gets a job at a talent agency. There, she meets agent Lyon Burke, played by Paul Burke of *Twelve O'Clock High* fame. Anne falls hard for Lyon but he wants something different from life than Anne, which eventually breaks them up.

Time goes by, and Anne appears in television commercials advertising products as the Gillian Girl. At this point, she and Lyon reunite. Their happiness doesn't last long because Neely O'Hara, played by Patty Duke, verbally seduces Lyon as her agent to go back to New York and support her comeback in a new play. Anne sees newspaper headlines in the gossip column about the two that leads to an emotional breakdown and now she is hooked on dolls After hitting rock bottom, Anne straightens herself out and leaves the Hollywood limelight for good. With her strength and dignity returned, she is strong enough to say no when Lyon comes back and proposes.

Neely O'Hara was a very different role for Patty Duke, and it helped her to escape the teenybopper image of her television series *The Patty Duke Show* in a big way. Her character is ambitious and does what she has to on her way to the top. Nothing will get in her way and keep her from stardom. After her relationship with Mel, played by Martin Milner *(Adam 12)* comes to an end, things start to spiral out of control. She gets hooked on dolls after going through some bad experiences. Eventually, she tries to get clean, but the dolls win and she suffers the consequences in the end.

Sharon Tate plays Jennifer North, a chorus girl who values her beauty over everything and works as an actress for a paycheck. Her life changes when nightclub singer Tony Polar, played by Tony Scotti, serenades her in front of her escort. It was love at first sight, and they became inseparable. They eventually get married, much to Tony's sister Miriam's (Lee Grant) disappointment. Miriam knows a tragic secret about Tony — he has Huntington's chorea. Miriam tells Jennifer about Tony's disease.

Jennifer is devastated when the secret is revealed, and she confides in Miriam that she's pregnant. Worried that the baby will inherit the genetic disease, Jennifer has an abortion. To take care of Tony's medical bills she ends up working in French art films. To continue Jennifer's tragic string of luck, she discovers she has breast cancer. This last blow is too much, and Jennifer takes an overdose of dolls to end her life.

Valley of the Dolls was released in America on December 15th 1967, after a major promotional cruise tour showing the film in various exotic locations with the cast and crew on board. Sharon received a Golden Globe nomination for her role as Jennifer for most promising newcomer.

Original (final draft) script for *Valley of the Dolls*

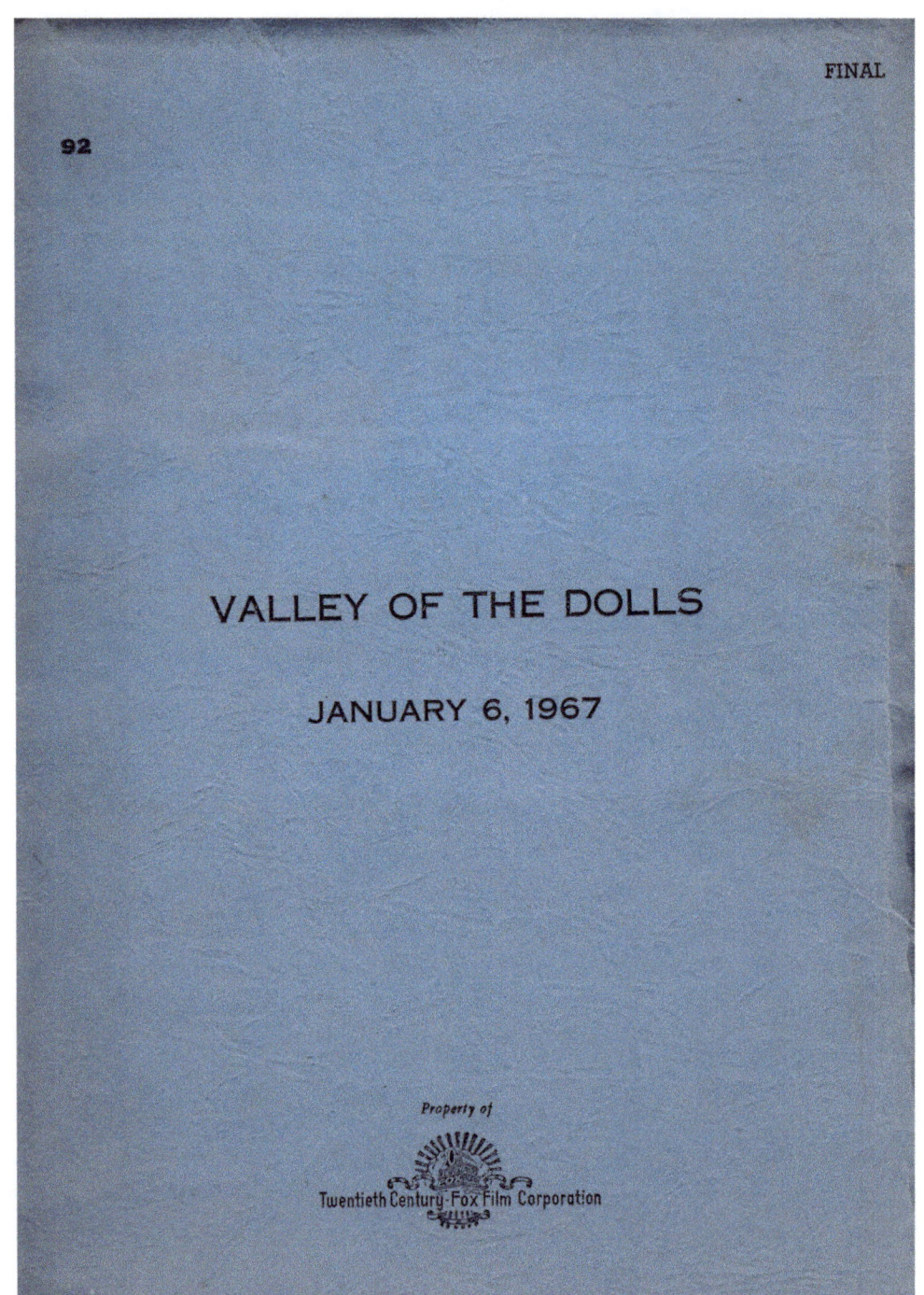

Original rare one of a kind hand-drawn and signed Travilla sketch showing Sharon as Jennifer North in a nightgown

This sketch can be seen on the wall during Jacqueline Susann's visit with Travilla when he was doing the fashion drawings for the actors in Valley of the Dolls *in the documentary,* Jacqueline Susann and the Valley of the Dolls, *released in 1967.*

Original set decoration painting showing the theatre where Jennifer (Sharon) is featured in a adult film

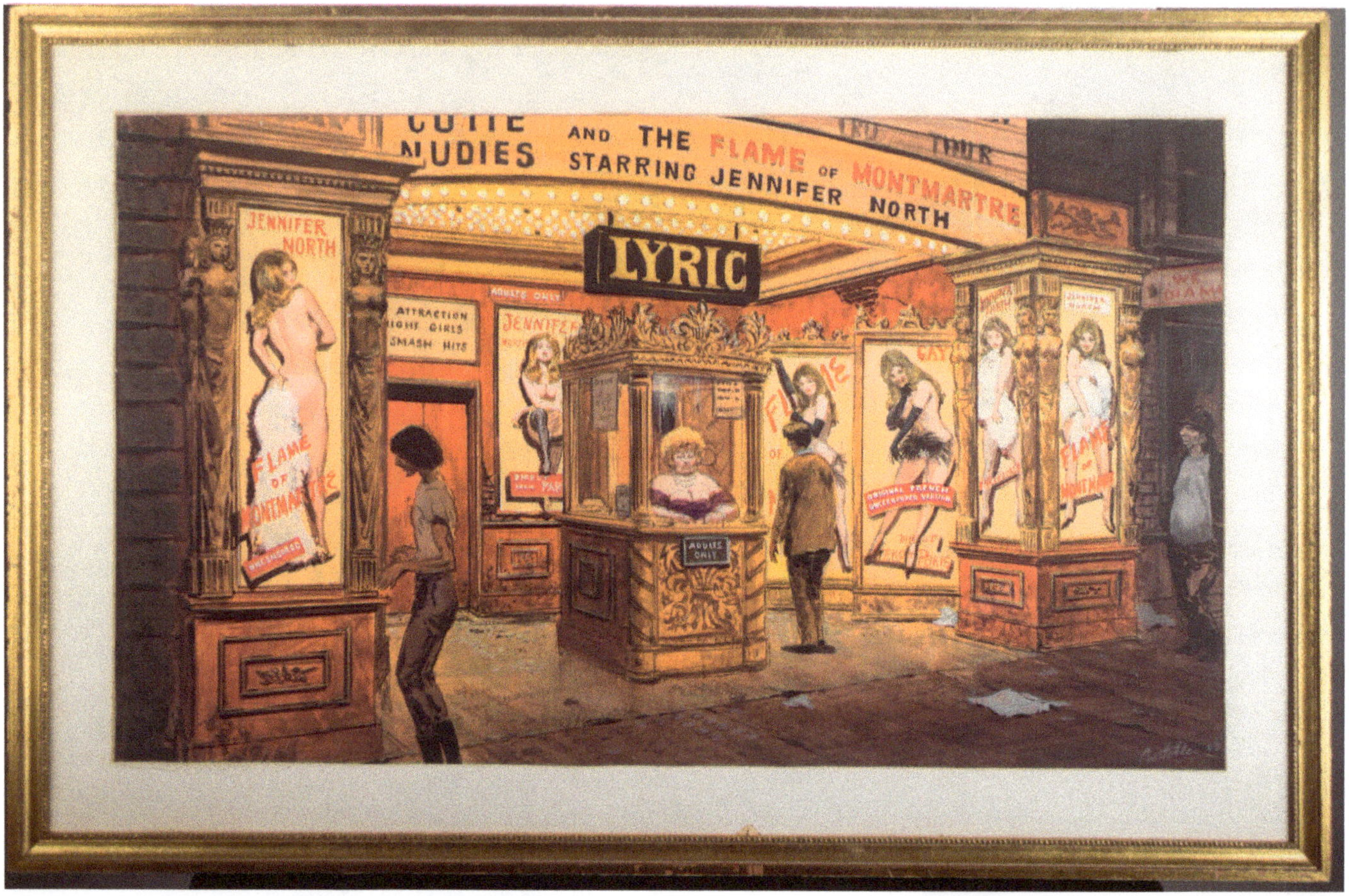

Actual painting can be seen when Jacqueline Susann is visiting the different sets in the documentary Jacqueline Susann and the Valley of the Dolls, *released in 1967.*

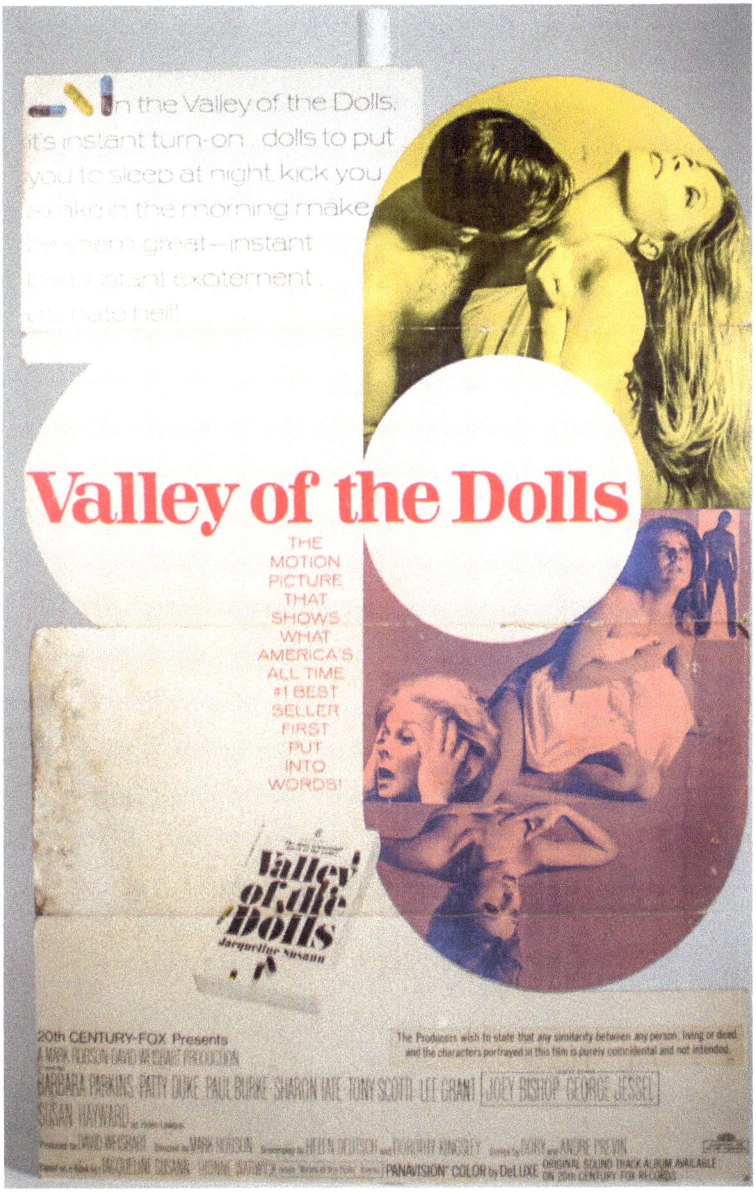

Valley of the Dolls Promotional Radio Spot Announcements from 20th Century Fox.

Valley of the Dolls very rare movie lobby stand up display used to promote the movie, they were placed at the front of the lobby or at the theatre entrance.

Very rare *Valley of the Dolls* soundtrack album signed by Sharon Tate, Barbara Parkins and Patty Duke

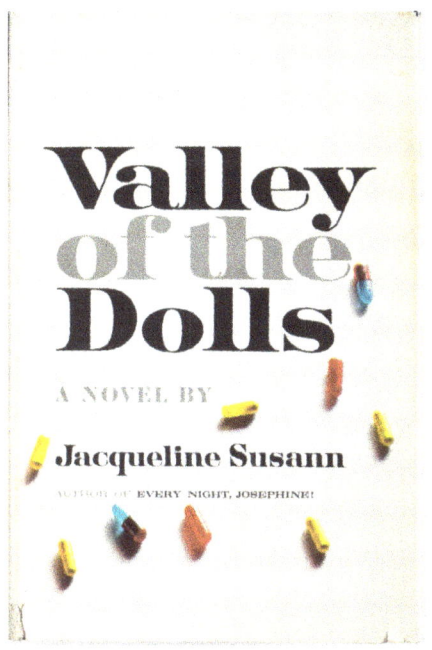

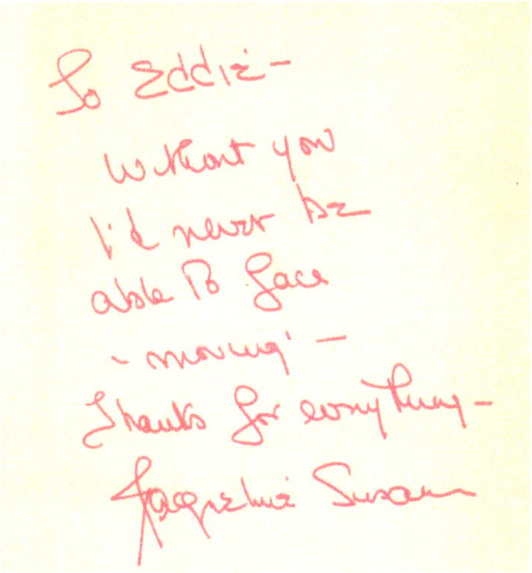

Valley of the Dolls *hardback book signed by author Jacqueline Susann.*

Original master file from 20th Century Fox featuring all the 8x10 lobby stills for all regions of the United States, press information on the cast and the synopsis of the movie.

International mini program and ticket for screening of Valley of the Dolls *in 1968.*

Very rare questionnaire rating the movie, cast, and likes and dislikes that was handed out to the audience attending a pre-screening (before release) of Valley of the Dolls.

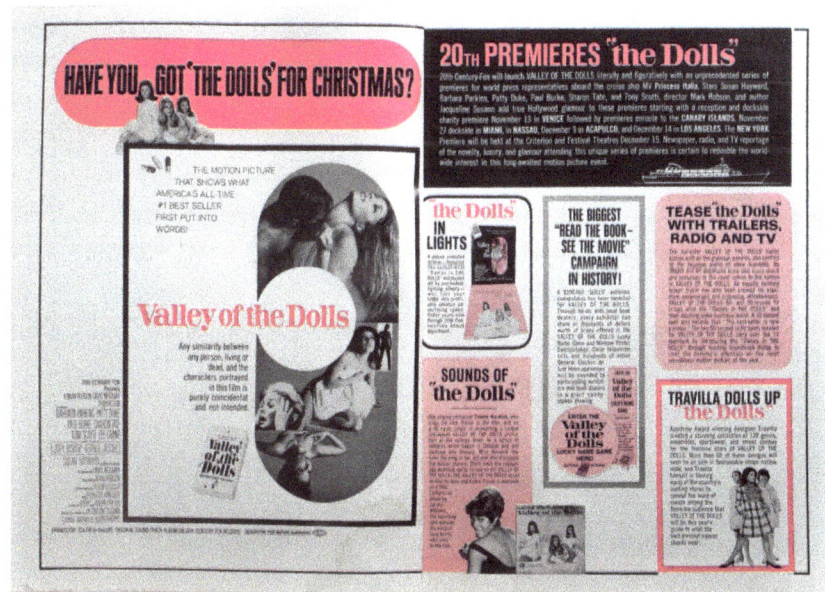

Original advertisement from December 4th 1967 issue of Box Office Magazine *promoting the world premiere of* Valley of the Dolls.

Movie posters, lobby cards and programs (US and foreign) for *Valley of the Dolls*

Original Japanese poster and movie program sold at theaters for Valley of the Dolls.

Very rare original 16 x 20 lobby card featuring Sharon Tate, Barbara Parkins and Patty Duke.

Music from the *Valley of the Dolls*

Reel to reel soundtrack tape.

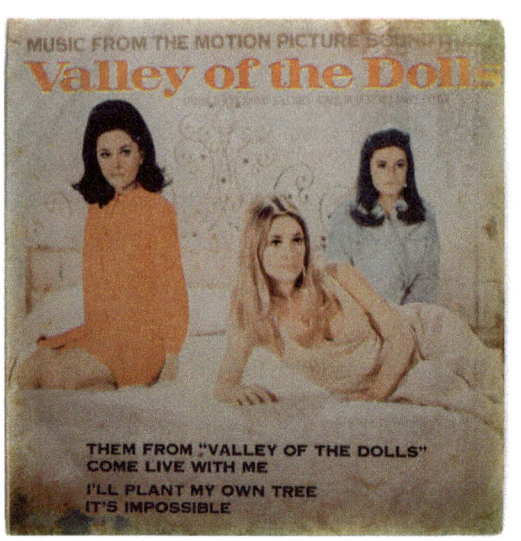

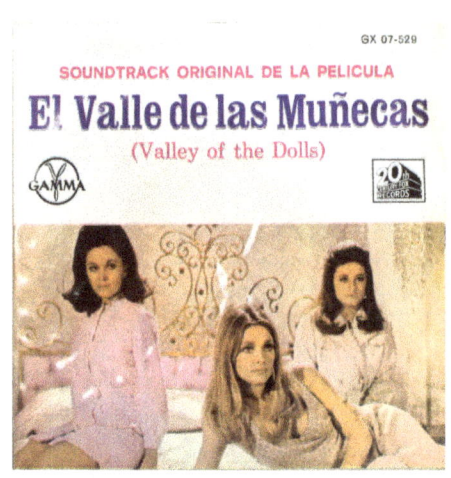

7" extended plays.

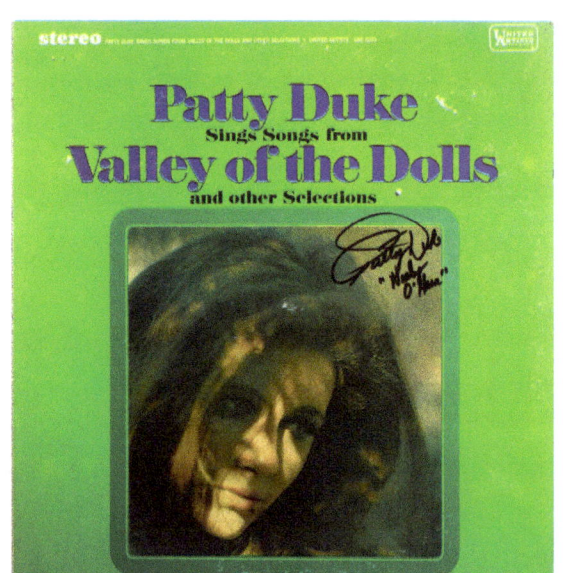

Patty Duke (Neely O'Hara) sings songs from Valley of the Dolls *signed by Patty Duke.*

8-track tape soundtrack.

Valley of the Dolls *sheet music signed by Barbara Parkins (Anne Welles).*

Fashion of the *Valley of the Dolls*

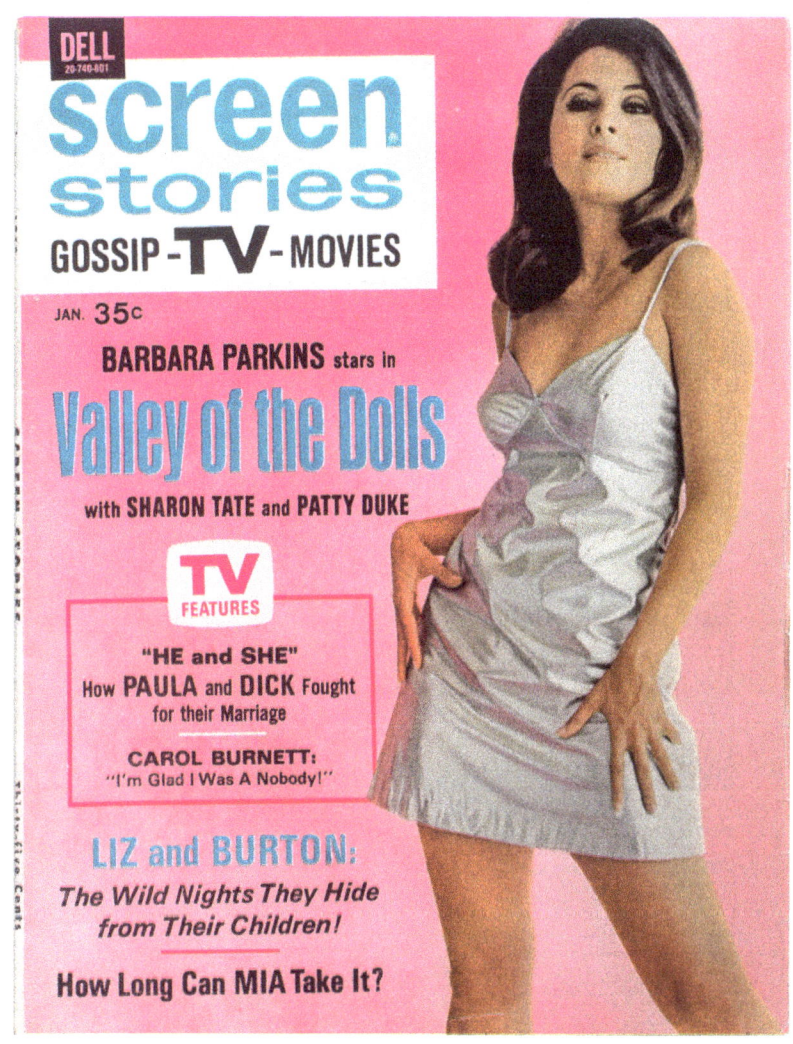

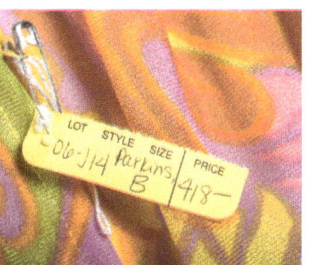

Barbara Parkins personally owned and worn dress from 1967.

Costume collection—
1967 Jody T mini dress worn by an extra
in Valley of the Dolls.

Cast members signed from *Valley of the Dolls*

Sharon Tate autograph from 1967.

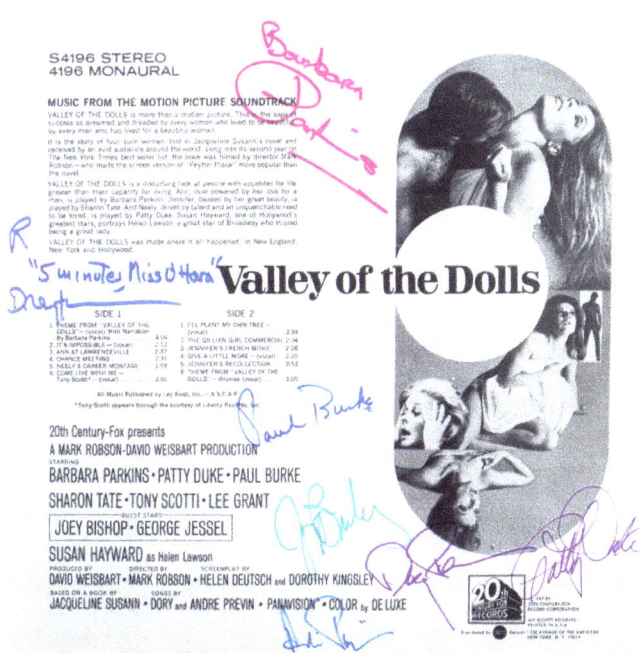

Valley of the Dolls *soundtrack album cover signed on the reverse by Barbara Parkins (Anne Welles), Patty Duke (Neely O'Hara), Paul Burke (Lyon Burke), Joey Bishop (himself), Andre Previn (composer), Dor Previn (composer), Richard Dreyfuss (extra—not credited, his first feature film).*

Susan Hayward (Helen Lawson) signed NBC photo session agreement signed by Hayward and NBC representative. The contract was signed in December 1967, the same month Valley of the Dolls *premiered.*

Valley of the Dolls *special widescreen edition (long out of print) laser disc set from CBS FOX Home Video was released in 1990. At the Hollywood Collectors Show in Los Angeles I met Barbara Parkins and Patty Duke and had both actresses autograph my laser disc cover with their character names below their signatures at my request.*

Autographs

Sharon Tate Hollywood the 60s original promotional photograph autographed by the photographer, Allan Grant (1919–2008). He was also a journalist for Life Magazine. I am really fortunate to have this signed photo in my collection. Only a few ever surfaced.

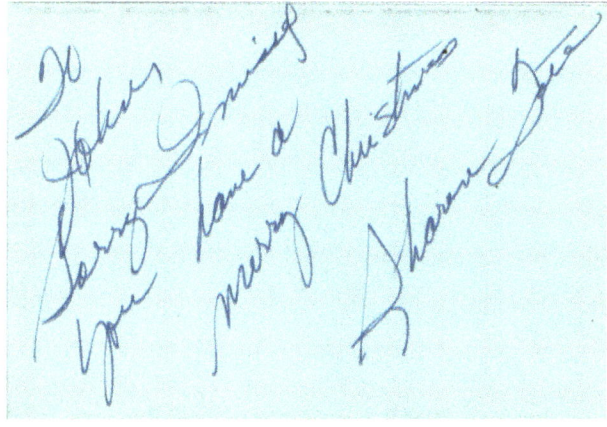

Above is a nice autograph from Sharon, who took extra time and wrote more than just her signature, including a nice holiday greeting. Uncommon in this form.

My definition of love is being full.
Complete.
It makes everything lighter.
Beauty is something you see.
Love is something you feel.

– Sharon Tate

"What I want out of life is happiness.
I don't want money. …
I like myself. I'm glad I'm me.
I'd like to have a baby."

– Sharon Tate

In 1968, after their wedding in January and settling in their home in London, Roman and Sharon remained on the go, jet-setting back and forth from London to Los Angeles to attend movie premieres, parties, etc. In May, they attended the Cannes Film Festival in France.

Back in Los Angeles by June and without a permanent residence, they stayed at the Chateau Marmont, a hotel. They stayed here on several occasions. They arrived at the hotel and Sharon filled out the guest registration card when checking in. (See below.)

Sharon returned in preparation for rehearsals, photo shoots, etc. for her next film titled, *The Wrecking Crew.* It featured Dean Martin as secret agent Matt Helm. This was Deans' fourth and final film in the series. Dean's co-star, along with Sharon who plays Freya, is the lovely Elke Sommer who plays Linka, the seductive villain.

A very rare registration card from the Chateau Marmont in Los Angeles filled out by Sharon as Mr.+ Mrs. Roman Polanski with their current address in London before moving to Cielo Drive.

The Wrecking Crew (House of 7 Joys)

Filming from July- August 1968

Release dates: Canada, Christmas Day 1968 • U.S. February 5, 1969

Sharon's Character: Freya Carlson

    The Wrecking Crew was an American comedy spy-fi film starring Dean Martin as Matt Helm with Elke Sommer, Nancy Kwan, Tina Louise and Sharon Tate, who portrays Frey Carlson. She is Matt's beautiful but rather clumsy travel guide from the Danish tourism bureau. Unknown to Matt Freya, it's later discovered she is a top-secret agent using a clever disguise. Sharon's comedic talents shine in her role as Freya. Elke Sommer plays the seductive Linka and Nancy Kwan plays Yu-Rang, both are accomplices for the villain of the film, Count Contini, played by Nigel Green.

    A highlight is a fight scene between Yu-Rang and Freya that was choreographed by martial arts expert and actor Bruce Lee. In the end, Matt saves the day and gets the girl — the very seductive Freya. However, while on the train as they embrace, Freya pulls the brake, they fly forward and the scene freezes. It is all in good fun, especially when Dean Martin is involved. Dean and Sharon had great chemistry together, and Elke Sommer became a good friend of Sharon's after filming.

    The Wrecking Crew premiered at the box office on December 25, 1968, released by Columbia Pictures.

Original hand-painted story board artwork featuring Sharon Tate (Freya Carlson), Dean Martin (Matt Helm), and Nancy Kwan (Yu-Rang). It is amazing this even survived since it was created over 50 years ago.

**Sharom Tate's personally owned and used script.
She signed her name at the top and added her character name, Freya.
Inside are several pages with handwritten notes by Sharon.**

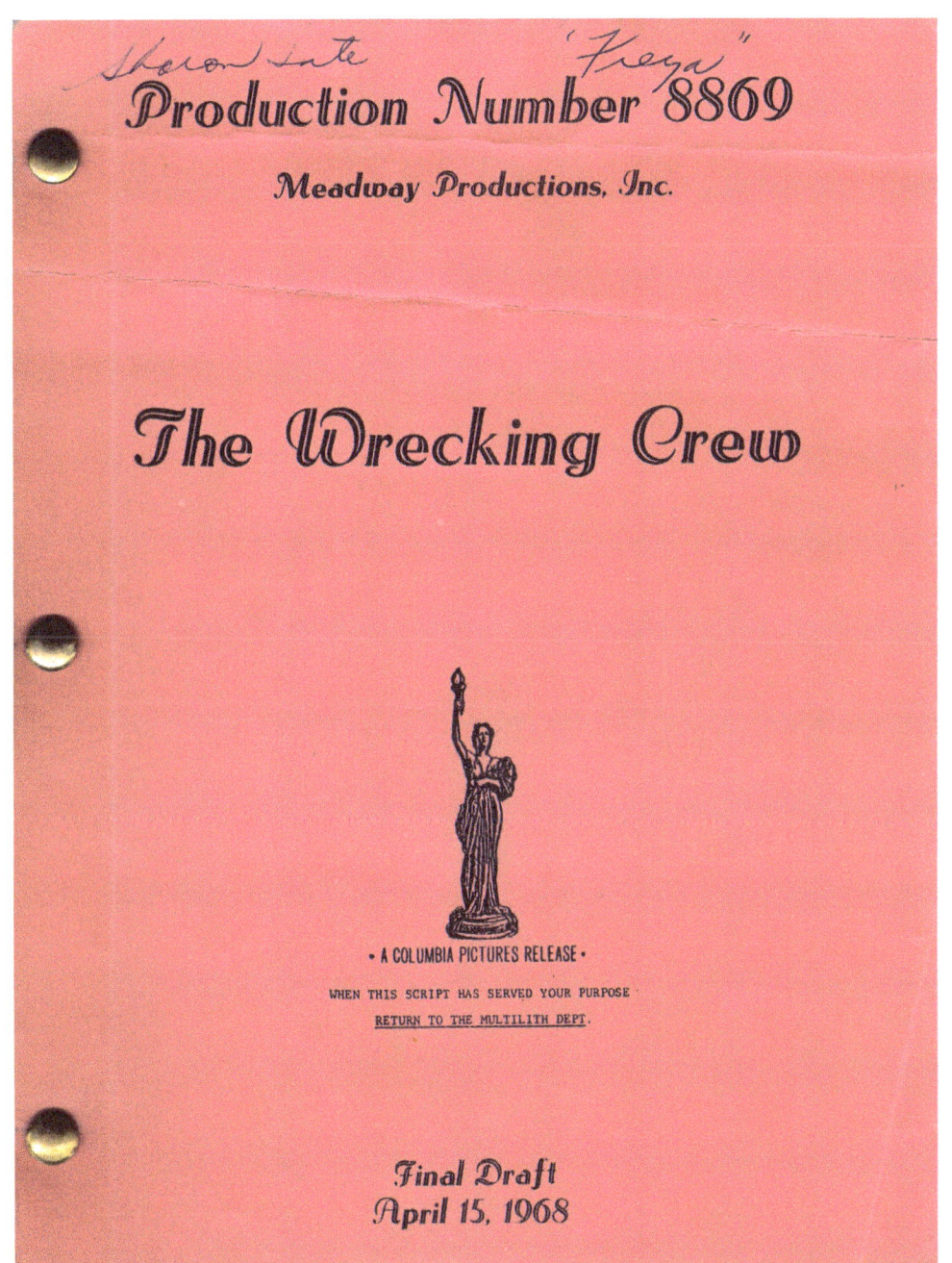

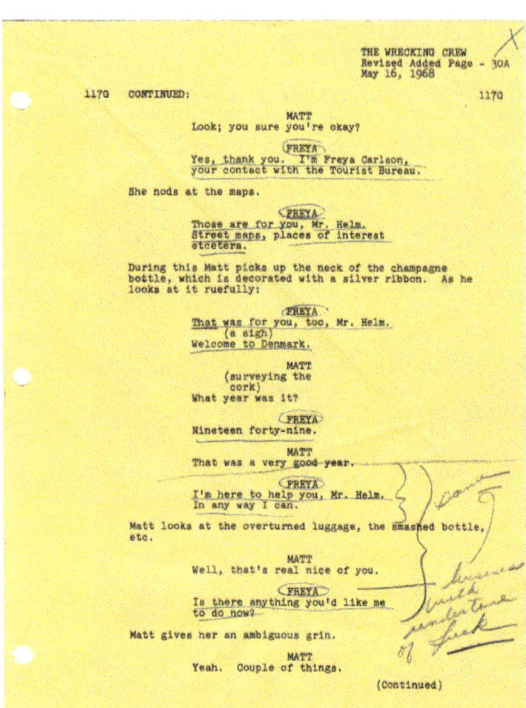
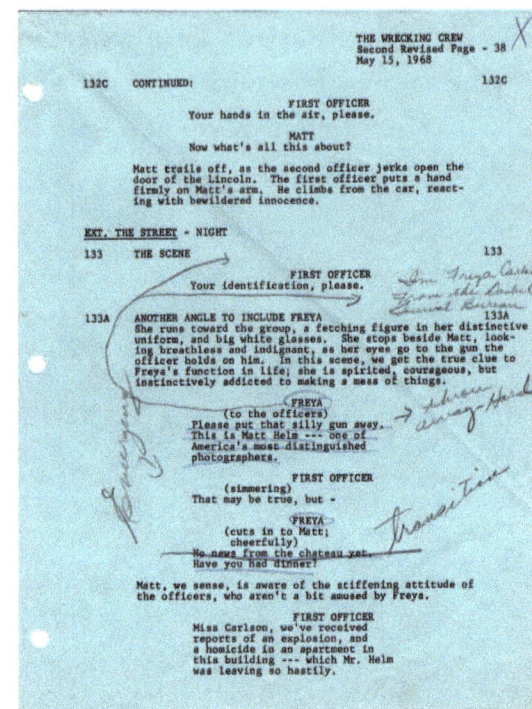
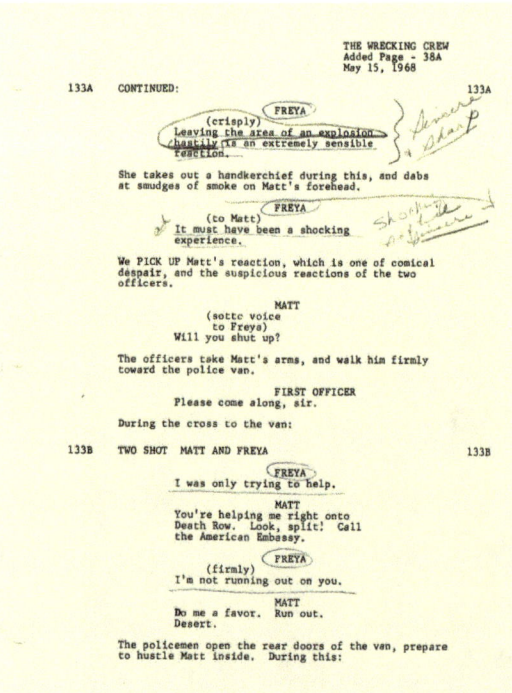
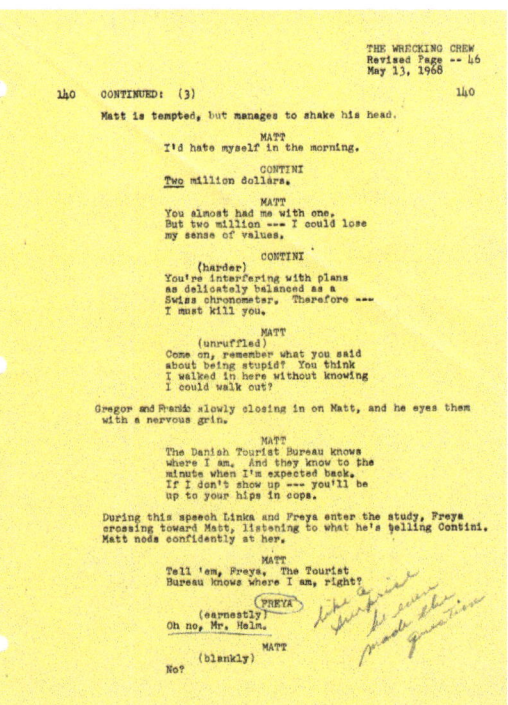

Sharon's personally owned and used shooting schedule that accompanied her script

```
                                                          EASTMAN COLOR
     PROD. NO. 8869   TITLE      THE WRECKING CREW (MEADWAY CLAUDE PROD)      PAGE  1
     DIRECTOR   PHIL KARLSON      PRODUCER  IRVING ALLEN      ART DIR   JOE WRIGHT
     BREAKDOWN ASST.  JERRY SIEGEL            SCRIPT DATED          4-15-68
     SCHED. DAYS 41 & 1  START DATE   7-16-8   FINISH DATE 8-27-68    TYPED 5-31-68
     HOLIDAY & 4 DAYS 2ND UNIT          SHOOTING SCHEDULE
```

DATE	SET	PAGES	SEQ.	SC'N'S	CAST
1ST & 2ND DAYS MON 7-1 & TUES 7-2	STAGE #16 INT. CONTINI'S STUDY(D) SC: 5B Burn-in SC: 6 Contini looks at watch, then TV. SC: 7A Burn-in SC: 8 Contini looking at monitors SC: 9 Linka gives command into mike on Contini signal. 25 Watching monitor-day behind schedule. SC: 31 Contini on mike gives command to intercept MacDonald. SC: 63 Contini on phone tells of gold-Linka watching men finish putting gold in pile.	2 2/8		3	Contini,Linka,Gregor,Frankie Karl 1 guard bit,4 guards extras sc 63,watch,4 carts, Efx: Burn in on monitor
	INT. CONTINI'S STUDY(D) SC: 90B Contini talks to Yu Rang over monitor. SC: 95 Contini answers phone SC: 96 Men finish bringing in gold-men spray gold w/paint. SC: 97 Contini on phone SC: 98 Linka enters-Contini hangs up phone-men spraying gold-they discuss Matt	2		32	Contini,Linka,Gregor Frankie, Karl 1 guard bit 2 men extras, 2 painters extras,gold ingots, paint cylinders w/hose,sc 90B-burn-in
	TOTAL PAGES	4 2/8			

Promotional materials for *The Wrecking Crew* and a very rare cast-autographed album page including Sharon Tate, Elke Sommer and Dean Martin (DM)

Mat 1A; Still No. 2
Dean Martin again stars as Matt Helm, the world's greatest agent, in "The Wrecking Crew," an Irving Allen production for Columbia Pictures release in Technicolor. Also starred are Elke Sommer, Sharon Tate, Nancy Kwan, Nigel Green and Tina Louise. Phil Karlson directed "The Wrecking Crew."

Mat 1D; Still No. 18
Elke Sommer is one of the kiss-and-kill lovelies who tangle with Dean Martin as Matt Helm in "The Wrecking Crew," new Irving Allen production for Columbia Pictures release in Technicolor. Others are Sharon Tate, Nancy Kwan and Tina Louise; Nigel Green also stars. Phil Karlson directed "The Wrecking Crew."

Mat 1E; Still No. 11
Sharon Tate may be on the side of Dean Martin as Matt Helm in "The Wrecking Crew"... maybe! Elke Sommer, Nancy Kwan, Nigel Green and Tina Louise also star in the new comedy adventure, an Irving Allen production for Columbia Pictures release in Technicolor.

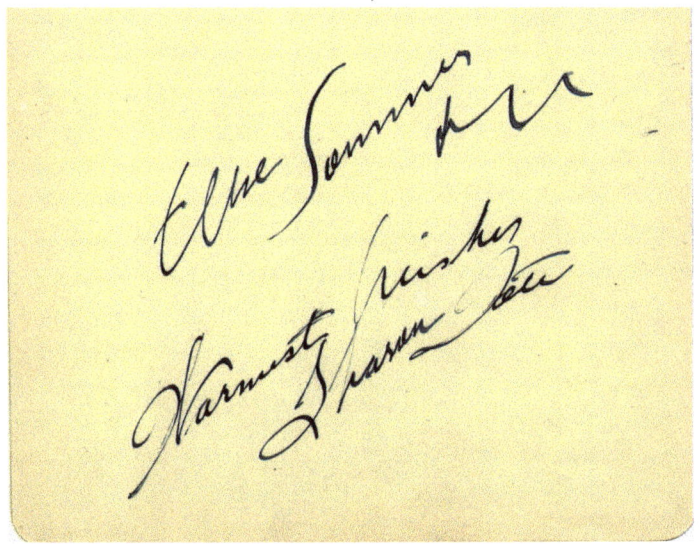

Original movie posters and lobby cards (US and foreign) for *The Wrecking Crew*

Window card with blank area at top so the location, date and time of the movie can be filled in and set inside business windows

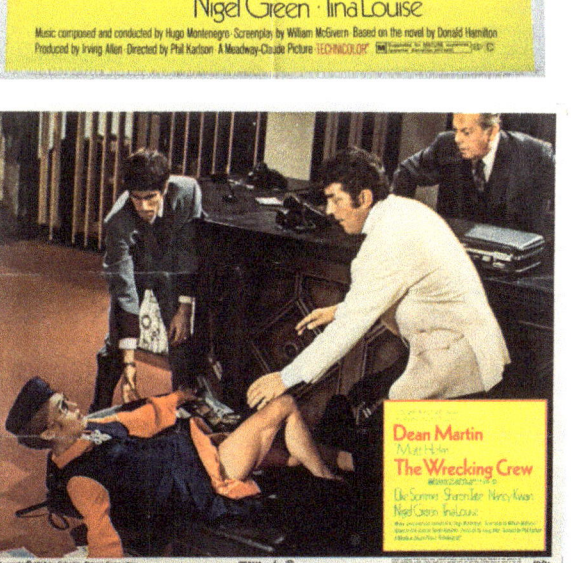

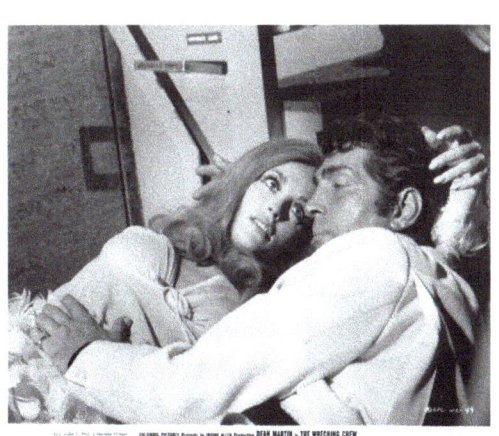

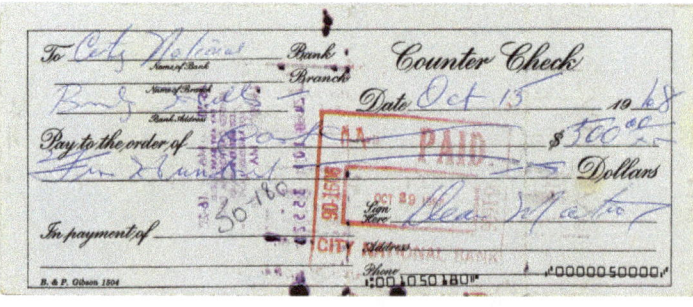

US half sheet (cardboard) movie poster measuring 22 x 28.

Dean Martin (Matt Helm) completely filled out and signed counter check from October 1968, the same time The Wrecking Crew *was being filmed.*

*Elke Sommer (Linka Karensky) signed
8 x 10 publicity photo from
The Wrecking Crew.*

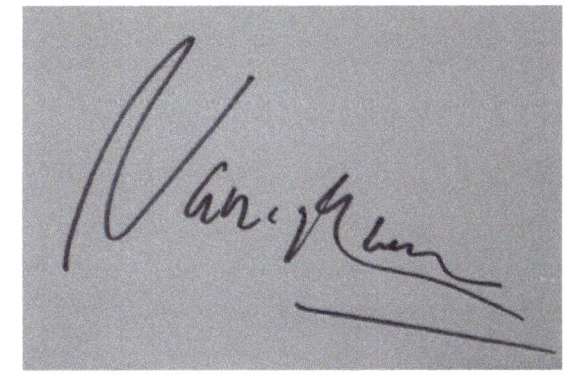

*Nancy Kwan (Yu-Rang)
autographed card.*

*"Beauty is only a look.
It has nothing to do with what I'm like inside."
– Sharon Tate*

Art & Publications

*"If you just take it down to bare facts,
the reason for living is the reason you make it.
I mean the brain was made to create."*
— *Sharon Tate*

PHOTOGRAPHS OF

Sharon Tate

BY

Walter Chappell

WITH AN ESSAY

BY RICHARD HOWARD

Sharon Tate by Mike Chappell rare limited edition book released in 2001.

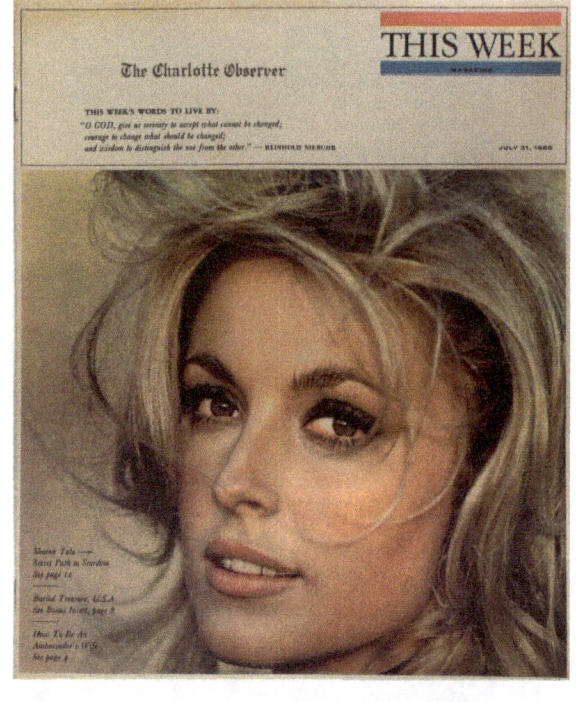

Esquire magazine from December 1967, featuring Sharon in a photo spread and story

"I can't play games.
I have friends, older women,
who tell me I'm foolish to let Roman know how deeply I care about him.
They tell me all sorts of things like 'keep a man guessing,'
'men become bored with too much devotion.'
They tell me I am being foolish.
Well, foolish I am."

– Sharon Tate

As quoted in *New Castle News* (9 December 1967)

"I'm just me.

If I am sexy, it's just something I do naturally,

like picking up a knife and fork to eat.

I think people who try to be sexy are the most unsexy people in the world."

– Sharon Tate

12 + 1 (The Thirteen Chairs)

Filming from March-May 1969

Italy release, October 7, 1969 • New York City release, May 1, 1970 • US release, August 15, 1970

Sharon's Character: Pat

    12+1 (Original title and Italian release title: *The Thirteen Chairs*) was a comedy based on the 1928 film titled *The Twelve Chairs*. The film starred Sharon Tate and Vittorio Gassman, with a special cameo appearance by Orsen Welles. The story begins with Mario (Gassman) rushing to England where he learns that his inheritance consists of only thirteen antique chairs of a certain value. He sells them to cover his transportation costs, but soon learns from his Aunt Laura's last message that a fortune in jewels is hidden in one of the chairs. He tries to buy them back, but is unsuccessful. He enlists the help of lovely American antiques dealer Pat (Sharon Tate), who works in the antiques shop in front of his Aunt Laura's house where he sold the chairs. The two set off on a bizarre quest for the chairs that takes them from London to Paris and Rome. Along the way, they meet a bizarre characters as they track down each chair. Through a process of elimination and a series of mishaps and mayhem, they end up in Rome where the final chair containing the jewels. It's on a truck and is collected by nuns who auction it off for charity. The movie concludes with Pat waving goodbye to Mario as he heads back to New York City.

    The movie was filmed from March to May 1969. The director had to use props to cover Sharon's pregnancy as the filming progressed. This was Sharon's final film before she headed home to the States to prepare for the arrival of her baby.

    The film was first shown in Italy on October 7, 1969, and then in New York in May 1970. It went nationwide in August 1970. The film was distributed by Avco Embassy Pictures. This was Sharon's final film.

 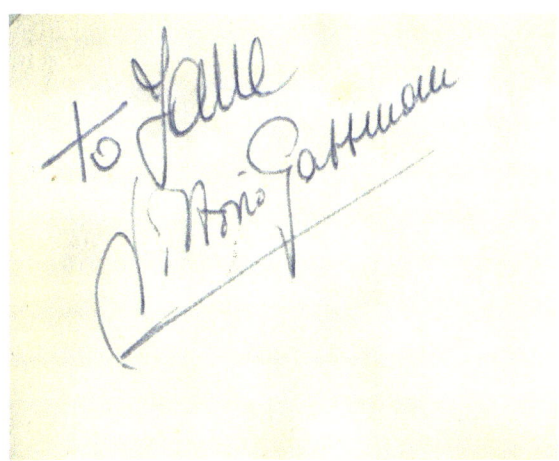

The stars of the movie signed autograph book pages.
Here are pages signed in July 1969 by a very pregnant Sharon Tate and her co-star Vittorio Gassman.
This was signed right before Sharon's return to the United States.

Promotion Materials From Italy For *12+1*

SHARON TATE PLUS RAVISSANTE QUE JAMAIS
DANS "12 + 1"
AVEC VITTORIO GASSMAN ET ORSON WELLES

SCENARIO

Dans un très modeste salon de coiffure pour hommes à New York, Mario, un émigré italien aux Etats-Unis, mène une vie difficile. Il reçoit la visite de son homme d'affaires qui l'informe de la mort de sa tante Laura qui vivait en Angleterre et dont il est le seul héritier. Mario part pour l'Angleterre. Malheureusement le "manoir" de sa tante n'est qu'une vieille baraque en ruine. La tante Laura a été contrainte de vendre presque tous ses biens et de prendre des hypothèques pour couvrir les dépenses de maladie et payer le fisc. De l'héritage il ne reste donc que la maison délabrée et 13 chaises : signées Hepplewhite. Mario décide de les vendre afin de pouvoir payer son voyage de retour aux Etats-Unis. L'antiquaire consulté estime leur valeur à 40 livres, mais lui demande de revenir le lendemain.
Derrière un portrait de sa tante, Mario trouve une lettre qui lui est destinée. Sa tante lui annonce que sa fortune est intacte et que 100.000 livres sont cachées dans la dernière chaise près de la fenêtre. Tout est là et sans impôts !
Mario se précipite donc chez l'antiquaire qui lui annonce triomphalement avoir vendu les treize chaises en un lot pour 100 livres... Mario exige le nom de l'acheteur que l'antiquaire refuse de lui communiquer : mais sa secrétaire, Pat, lui fait discrètement signe de le rejoindre. Elle lui donne le nom de l'acquéreur, Mr Bennet, moyennant le partage du butin. Entre Mario et Pat naît aussitôt une véritable idylle : ils se disputeront, se battront, s'aimeront... UNE ÉTOURDISSANTE FARANDOLE, COUPÉE D'INTERLUDES PASSIONNÉS
Dans la galerie d'art et l'antiquaire de Mr Bennet, Pat et Mario ne trouvent que huit chaises. Bennet en a vendu une à l'ambassadeur de Macabia à Paris, il en a donné deux à son médecin et le secrétaire de Bennet, un homosexuel, en a donné une à un propriétaire d'une boutique de mode en face de la galerie. Mario commence à lacérer une des huit chaises restantes chez Bennet lorsqu'il est surpris et jeté à la porte par le médecin.
Pendant ce temps, Pat s'est précipitée dans le magasin de mode où la chaise se trouve en vitrine. Mario l'y rejoint et pendant qu'il distrait la vendeuse, Pat lacère fébrilement la chaise sans se rendre compte qu'elle est vue par tous les passants. Le médecin de Bennet qui a déjà vu Mario s'attaquer aux chaises, les entraîne dans son cabinet de consultation, certain d'avoir découvert une nouvelle sorte de maladie mentale. Dans la salle d'attente du médecin, Mario "sonde" avec son rasoir l'une des chaises tandis que Pat ravira l'autre.
Tous deux réussissent à s'enfuir, persuadés que le trésor n'est dans aucune des chaises "visitées" jusqu'à présent. Le "génial" Markau lui présente une pièce d'horreur a acheté deux chaises. Mario, se faisant passer pour un figurant, réussit à provoquer une incroyable pagaille sur la scène, deux malheureuses chaises sont lacérées sans succès et le spectacle d'horreur s'écroule, accompagné des rires de la salle.
Six chaises ont été examinées, il en reste donc sept : une à l'ambassade de Macabia à Paris et six à la galerie Bennet. Mario part pour Paris tandis que Pat se charge de Bennet. A l'ambassade, Mario découvre la chaise et fait une cour empressée à la jeune secrétaire noire qui "l'introduit" en pleine nuit dans l'ambassade. Il finit par éventrer une chaise de plus, sans résultat. Une fois de plus, Mario s'enfuit et regagne l'Angleterre. A Londres, il retrouve Pat. Bennet est mort et les chaises, parmi d'autres meubles, sont mises aux enchères. Pat et Mario participent à ces enchères et obtiennent... un buste d'Hepplewhite.
Après de nouvelles péripéties, ils arrivent dans une magnifique demeure sicilienne. La chaise contenant le trésor aboutit finalement chez la mère supérieure d'un orphelinat en Italie. Celle-ci découvre les 100.000 livres et croit au miracle. L'argent servira à reconstruire l'orphelinat... Mario renonce. L'Italie est belle, la propriété du Commendatore est vaste et confortable et lui-même est charmant : Pat décide de rester. Mario trouve une place de coiffeur sur un paquebot en partance pour New-York. A son arrivée aux Etats-Unis, il apprend qu'il a fait fortune, mais pas du tout dans le ventre d'une chaise !

UN GRAND TALENT COMIQUE

UN FILM QUI FERA LA JOIE DE TOUS LES VRAIS AMATEURS DE BONNE COMEDIE.

Sharon Tate omringd door internationale vedetten

SCENARIO

In "12 + 1" is Sharon Tate een verrukkelijke verkoopster in een antiekzaak. Ze maakt kennis met Vittorio Gassman — in de rol van Mario — en helpt hem een fabelachtige erfenis — die dreigt verloren te gaan — terug te vinden.
Mario, een bescheiden kapper van Italiaanse afkomst en wonend in New York, is naar Engeland overgekomen om te erven van tante Laura die zopas gestorven is. Daar wacht hem echter een grote ontgoocheling. In plaats van het prachtige kasteel zijner dromen, ondervindt Mike dat hij slechts een verschrikkelijke barak heeft geërfd.
Eigenlijk beperkt de ganse erfenis zich tot 13 stoelen, getekend Hepplewhite, die hij kwijtraakt bij de antiekzaak waar Sharon werkt.
Ondertussen heeft Mario-Gassman een brief gevonden die het onthutsende geheim — dat een van de stoelen 100.000 ponden bevat — prijsgeeft. Er blijft Mario dus maar één zaak te doen : kost wat kost die stoelen terug in zijn bezit krijgen.
Dan volgen wij Sharon en Gassman op een dolle jacht naar de stoelen. Dolle achtervolgingen, knettergekke situaties en frivole liefdestonelen zijn de ingrediënten van deze sprankelende film waarin Sharon Tate bewijst dat ze ook over een groot komisch talent beschikte.

ONVERWACHTE SITUATIES...

PIKANTE LIEFDESTONELEN...

SPEKTAKULAIRE ACHTERVOLGINGEN...

- Knettergek blijspel omtrent het geheim van 13 stoelen.
- Een ware hulde aan de levensblijheid van Sharon.
- Een ongelooflijke schaterlach met pit.
- Een opeenvolging van originele gags.
- Frisse filmkluif voor graaglachers.
- Dolle film vol fonkelende humor.
- 2 uur sprankelend ontspanningsgenot.
- Grappig, vrolijk maar vooral sexy.
- Welke man kan weerstaan aan zo'n vrouw ?
- U kunt zich aan alles verwachten in deze film.
- Een pittig blijspel, ondeugend en vol vaart.

12+1

Eine Filmkomödie in Farbe
mit Sharon Tate
Vittorio Gassman
Orson Welles
Vittorio de Sica
Mylène Demongeot

FILM FÜR SIE

12+1

21/72

137

Movie posters and lobby cards (foreign and US) for *12+1 / The Thirteen Chairs*

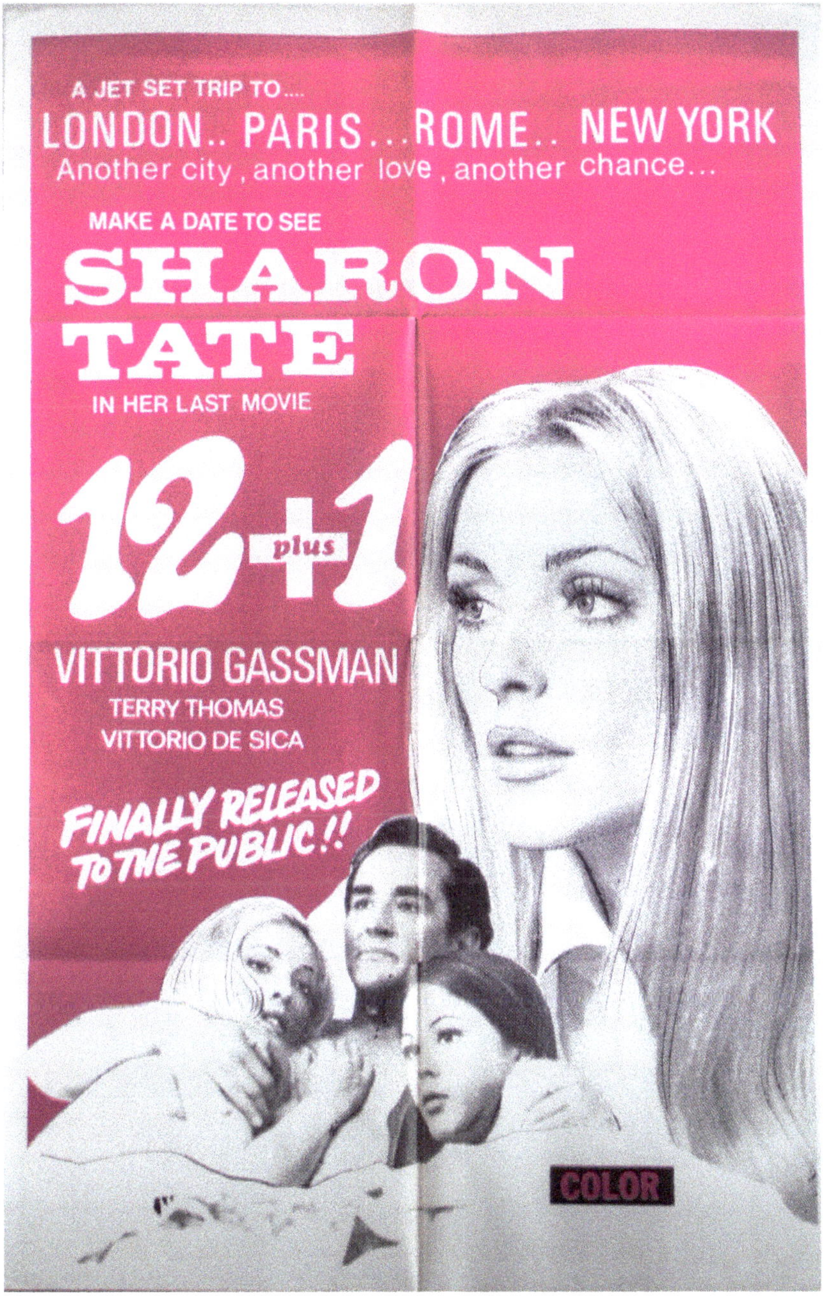
A JET SET TRIP TO....
LONDON.. PARIS...ROME.. NEW YORK
Another city, another love, another chance...
MAKE A DATE TO SEE
SHARON
TATE
IN HER LAST MOVIE
12 plus +1
VITTORIO GASSMAN
TERRY THOMAS
VITTORIO DE SICA
FINALLY RELEASED TO THE PUBLIC!!
COLOR

Cinema Teatro TRAETTA
VITTORIO GASSMAN - SHARON TATE
ORSON WELLES in
una su 13
con
OTTAVIA PICCOLO - JOHN STEINER - GREGOIRE ASLAN
TIM BROOKE TAYLOR - MARZIO MARGINE
CON LA PARTECIPAZIONE STRAORDINARIA DI
VITTORIO DE SICA - MYLENE DEMONGEOT - TERRY-THOMAS
REGIA DI
NICOLAS GESSNER E LUCIANO LUCIGNANI
TECHNICOLOR®
DISTRIBUZIONE ITALIAN INTERNATIONAL FILM

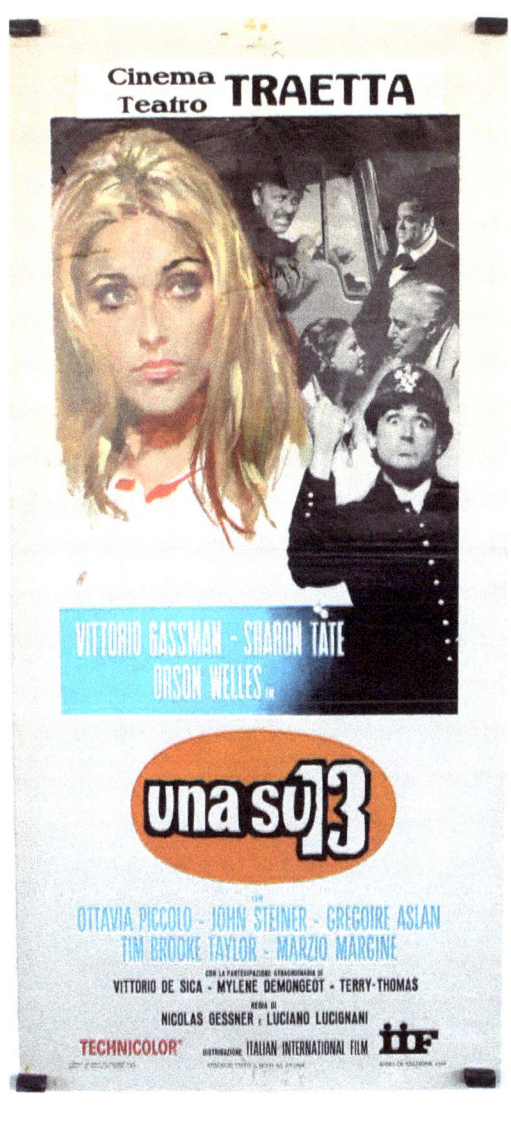

Home Video

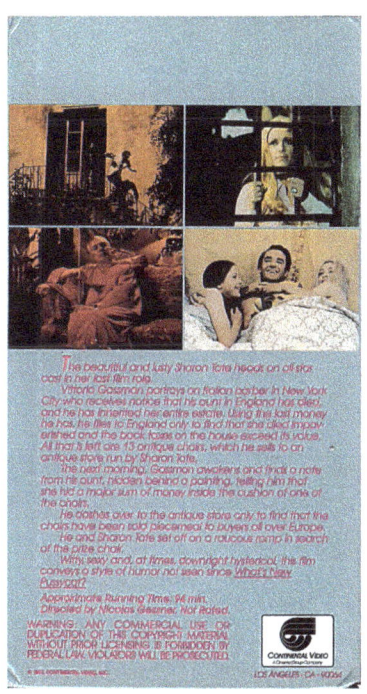

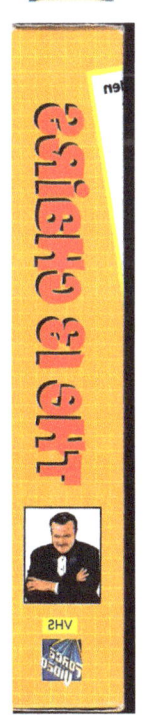

My Uncle Jack was an autograph collector his entire life. He lived in New York until the 1980's and spent all his spare time at stage doors, movie premiers, public signings and places frequented by celebrities, like Sardi's in New York. After moving to Florida, he used to work as an extra in locally filmed movies and *Miami Vice* episodes.

I apologize that I cannot give you specific information about the autograph, because Uncle Jack passed away two years ago. He had 2 of Sharon Tate's autographs, and I sold one of them last year. That one had an actual photograph of Sharon Tate attached to the back. I have sent you a copy of the photograph taken of Sharon Tate because I believe he received the autographs at the same time as the photograph. I wish there was more I could tell you, but that is all I know.

Thanks,
Linda Harmon

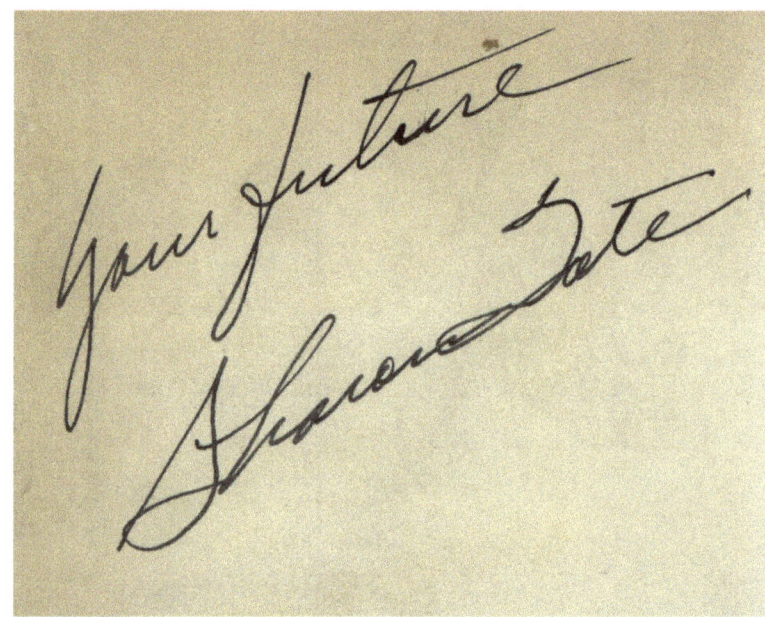

Friends

"They said they had a plan for me.
They would train me and prepare me.
I was immediately put into training–like a race horse.
I had a job to stay the way I was..."
– Sharon Tate

Sharon Tate had many friends over the years. Women as well as Men. Some were very close to her. I am paying hom-age and featuring some of those women that were a part of her life's journey.

On a personal note, I was fortunate to meet with friends and co-stars of Sharon's, including Tony Curtis, Martin Milner, Barbara Parkins, Max Baer, Patty Duke, and Susanna Leigh at events such as collector's shows, film festivals, etc. All were generous enough to share kind words and memories of Sharon in a warm hearted fashion.

– Tom Fontaine

Joanna Pettit

Joanna Pettit, the first thing comes to mind for me when I think of Joanna is strikingly beautiful and how she looked so much like Sharon especially in the 60s and 70s. Joanna, an actress in her own right, seeing her on screen, whether movies or television, I felt like she channeled Sharon in a way. Just recently I was watching an episode of Mannix starring Mike Connors and as I was watching Joanna on screen with her long blonde hair and hip fashion I could not get over how much she looks like Sharon! I even had to pause the screen a couple of times.

Joanna has been out of the public eye for sometime now but in the swinging 60s she was hanging out with Sharon and Roman along with her and then husband, actor Alex Cord.

Wende Wagner, best know as Miss Case in the ABC television show Green Hornet co-starring Bruce Lee, was one of Sharon's best friends starting in the mid-1960s.

She was married to actor Jim Mitchum (Robert's son) in 1966 and that marriage lasted over ten years. They had a son in 1969. I remember Jim when he played Eskimo Dobbs in one of my favorite movies, Ride the Wild Surf, *released in 1964.*

Wende left the business early, but for years she attended Collectors shows, signing autographs and telling stories. Sadly I never got a chance to meet her, as she passed away in 1997 from cancer.

Wende Wagner

Barbara Bouchet, who was born in Germany, is an actress with a long list of television and film credits from Hollywood to Italy. She also played Kelinda in the Star Trek *episode "By Any Other Name" in 1968. (See limited autograph card at left.)*

She was very good friends with Sharon. A blonde beauty herself, Barbara began her career as a model and then started an acting career that spans several decades. Most recently she appeared in the 2002 movie Gangs of New York, *starring Leonardo Dicaprio.*

Barbara would visit Sharon from time to time at her home and attending events, clubs, etc. Just recently, Barbara opened up about Sharon and released some great pictures of the two. Barbara is 79 years old now and owns a fitness club in Rome. I am sure she has many great memories of the time she spent with Sharon.

In 1964, Mia Farrow debuted as Allison MacKenzie, on the hit drama series Peyton Place, and that starring role launched her career. (At right is an early Peyton Place *promotional photo of Mia.)*

She and Sharon became friends when she was cast in director Roman Polanski's film Rosemary's Baby, which started filming in August of 1967 and finished in December of that year. Sharon was occasionally on set, since she had just completed filming the highly anticipated Valley of the Dolls in June.

Mia and Sharon remained friends after the film wrapped, and she attended the London premiere of Rosemary's Baby with the couple in January 1968, the same month they were married. Mia hung out with Sharon back in the states as well when she was filming The Wrecking Crew with Dean Martin, and later partied with her at Jay Sebring's house.

Mia Farrow

Barbara Parkins

Barbara Parkins played Betty Anderson in the hit drama Peyton Place, *and eventually tested for and starred in* Valley of the Dolls. *She and Sharon became friends during filming. They were so close that Sharon asked Barbara to be maid of honor in her wedding to Roman on January 20, 1968.*

On a personal note, I met Barbara in 2010 at a show and she was so kind and gracious too me. I told her I was a collector of Sharon Tate's memorabilia and she was fascinated by how I had been able to gather so many items. I could tell she was a bit private when it came to telling stories about her time with Sharon, so I respected that and didn't pressure her to share anything too personal. She offered me a chance to purchase her personal script from Valley of the Dolls *to add to my collection, but I could not afford it at the time. She graciously signed several items for me and I noticed she had a smile on her face as she viewed some of them. That was nice to see.*

Suzanna Leigh

Suzanna Leigh, a retired British actress who appeared in movies with Elvis Presley, Tony Curtis, Jerry Lewis and many others throughout her career, was one of the women I spoke with on the phone about Sharon.

She remembered Sharon fondly, however she was not a big fan of Roman. She elaborated on those feelings, but she has since passed away so out of respect for her I will refrain from repeating anything negative and just say that she and Sharon were good friends.

Above is the note she sent me regarding Sharon's engagement ring, which she owned at the time I met her. For some reason, she wrote the note to Jim and not Tom. Oh well, she was a nice person and was kind to me. I was sad to learn she left us on December 11, 2017.

Sheilah Wells

Sheilah/Sheila was best friends with Sharon. In the 1960s, the two actresses shared an apartment in LA.

When Sheilah gave birth to her daughter, she gave her the middle name "Tate" and asked Sharon to be her Godmother.

"I think the greatest thing I could say about Sharon was that she was for real. I mean really for real."
— Sheliah Wells

Roman is such a beautiful, mad human being. Sometimes things are difficult, sometimes good. But it makes life twice as interesting."

— Sharon Tate

Autographed 5 x 7 publicity photo signed to a fan in 1969 who requested an autograph from Sharon through the mail.

She graciously signed it herself with a previously stamped autograph and personalized it to Irene.

What makes this personally special to me is Irene resided in my home town of Indianapolis.

On January 2, 1969 Sharon signed a new contract with S.G.F. Enterprises for exclusive services as actress in motion pictures and accepting employment for future films, etc.

January was a very happy month for Sharon especially knowing that she was expecting her first child with Roman, celebrated their First Year Wedding anniversary on the 20th, attending the London Premiere of *Rosemary's Baby* on the 23rd directed by her husband and celebrating her 26th birthday the day after.

```
                    S G F ENTERPRISES, INC.
                c/o Schwartzman, Greenberg & Fimberg
                       9777 Wilshire Boulevard
                       Beverly Hills, CA 90212


                           January 2, 1969




        Miss Sharon Tate
        10050 Cielo Drive
        Beverly Hills, California

        Dear Miss Tate:

                This will constitute the following agreement between
        us:

                1.  We hereby employ and engage you to render your exclusive
        services for us as an actress in motion pictures; and you here-
        by accept such employment and agree to keep and perform all of
        your obligations and agreements hereunder.  Your services here-
        under shall include such other services as may be required of
        actresses according to the custom of the industry.

                2.  You agree that throughout the term hereof you will render
        your services solely and exclusively for us; that you will promptly
        and faithfully comply with all reasonable instructions, directions,
        requests, rules and regulations made or issued by us, and that you
        will perform your services conscientiously and to the full limit of
        your ability at all times, when and wherever required or desired by
        us and as instructed by us in all matters, including those involving
        artistic taste and judgment.  Your said services shall be rendered
        for us at all times with due regard to a prompt, efficient and
        economical production of motion pictures.  You agree that you will
        not at any time during the term hereof render any services of any
        kind to or for any person, firm or corporation other than ourselves,
        except in connection with so-called "loanouts" as hereinafter pro-
        vided.

                3.  The term of your employment hereunder shall be deemed
        to commence on January 3, 1969, and shall continue for a period
        of one (1) year thereafter, provided we shall have an option for
        an additional one (1) year period.

                                                                     1.
```

17. This agreement shall be construed in accordance with the laws of the State of California.

If the foregoing is in accordance with your agreement and understanding please so indicate by signing this agreement below.

                                      Very truly yours,

                                      S G F ENTERPRISES, INC.

                                      By: _____

ACCEPTED:

_____
Sharon Tate

Roman and Sharon were out and about in Hollywood, attending film premieres, events, etc. up until it was time for them to leave the country for their respective projects. She was heading to Rome to star in *The Thirteen Chairs* later titled *12+1,* which started filming in March. They had to do some tricky camera work for this film, as Sharon was more than four months pregnant and was starting to show towards the end of filming.

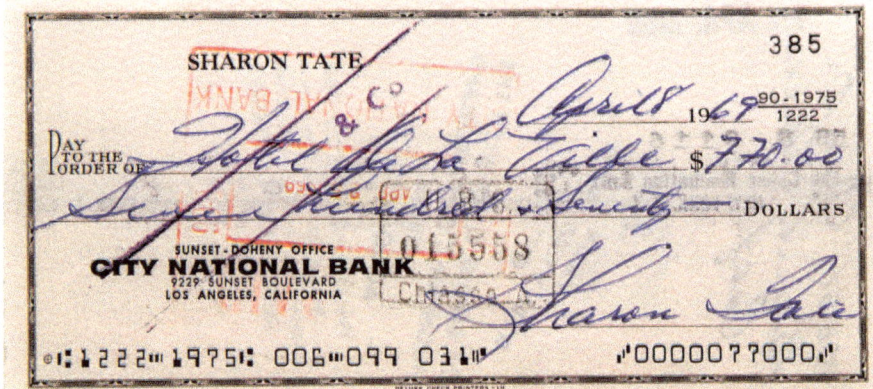

Incredibly rare check completely filled out and signed by Sharon to the Hotel De La Ville in Italy. She stayed there while filming on location for her final film, 12+1/The 13 Chairs, *with Vittorio Gassman. She has also added her home address, 10050 Cielo Drive, Beverly Hills, Calif. on the reverse side.*

Sharon's Heart of Gold

After filming was done in Italy for *12+1/The 13 Chairs*, Sharon returned to England. In July, she packed her bags to head back to Los Angeles to the couple's new residence at 10050 Cielo Drive in Beverly Hills so she could prepare for the birth of their first child due in late August. Roman was still scouting film locations and could not leave, so he drove Sharon to Southampton with her dog Prudence and she boarded the *Queen Elizabeth II* for the voyage home.

At the beginning of Sharon's voyage back to Los Angeles on the *QE 2*, a very special moment happened, and only one living person knew about it until I acquired the letter and its artifacts shown on the following page. The items and letter speak for themselves and add a new chapter to what happened during Sharon's voyage back to the States.

Letter of Provenance

This item comes from the personal collection of Helen Johnson of Los Angeles, California. Mrs. Johnson met actress Sharon Tate briefly on July 20, 1969. On that day, Sharon was arriving in Los Angeles from her return to London on the Queen Elizabeth II. Mrs. Johnson's son, Matthew, was afraid of swimming and he was uneasy to board the ship. Johnson was to meet her husband back in London. However, her boy was nervous as they approached the ship. That is when she saw Sharon Tate who was holding a puppy and a purse. Sharon took notice of Mrs .Johnson's son and Tate noticed that her son, Matthew was frightened. Sharon proceeded to ask her about her son and Johnson explained the situation while the boy eyed and petted Sharon's puppy. Johnson stated that Sharon was very pleasant and she offered the young boy a lace handkerchief with a sterling silver medal of St. Elmo. Tate told the young boy that the medal would protect him aboard the ship. She explained to Mrs. Johnson that Elmo was the Patron Saint of Sailors and that she had been given the medal before boarding the Queen Elizabeth II ship herself by a young sailor as a medal of protection and that, with Tate being pregnant, that the young sailor had offered it to her before she left London and that it had protected her during her own stay on the ship. It took a little convincing for the little fellow to accept and believe what Tate was saying. However, given Tate's kind nature and love of children, she was able to convince the youngster that all would be okay as long as he kept the medal with him. Mrs. Johnson thanked Tate profusely and the two parted ways.

Johnson never forgot the kind gesture from Tate and she kept the medal for decades after and only her family and close friends knew about the medal as Mrs. Johnson thought it would cause the press to pester her family for a story in the press. In addition, she was afraid that the medal might be stolen if anyone knew of it's existence.

Later, when Mrs. Johnson passed away her son kept it in his possession. It then came into the possession of another descent of the family.

Provenance of this collection: Formerly the collection of Helen Johnson, then by descent through the Johnson family.

This item is certified to be an original piece from The Helen Johnson Estate and is designated as:

The small lace handkerchief along with a St. Elmo's sterling silver medal once in the possession of actress Sharon Tate.

Sharon's lace handkerchief she gave to the little boy on the *QE2*

On the ship, Sharon did the usual things like shopping, dining, etc. — the typical things you would do to keep you occupied on a voyage that lasts several days. During the voyage, she also watched the launch of the Apollo 11 spaceship from the Kennedy Space Center in Florida on July 16.

Safely back at her home on July 20, she invited her parents and two sisters to spend the day and watch the historic lunar landing of Apollo 11 so they could see Neil Armstrong be the first man to walk on the moon. Friends Jay Sebring and house-sitters Abigail Folger and Wojciech Frykowski visited earlier that day.

Sharon, now very pregnant, was excited to be home and prepare to have her baby. She wished Roman was home as well, because she did have many friends who could check in on her from time to time.

As Sharon was settling back into normality, she visited Fuhrman's Furs in Beverly Hills on August 1, (my birthday). Her receipt, signed "Sharon Tate" in blue ink, shows a charge of $45 for a "clean and glaze" on both her fox and mink coats.

On August 8, 1969, Los Angeles was suffering from a very hot day. Sharon was more than 8-1/2 months pregnant and was feeling the heat more than anyone and spent most of the day relaxing at home. She did have some friends come over and check on her including her friend Joanna Pettit and Jay in the late afternoon. In the early evening, Jay, Abby, Wojciech and Sharon went out to dinner to the Coyote Mexican Restaurant on Beverly Blvd to have a nice meal and enjoy a nice evening together.

Sharon and Jay at Cielo Drive on August 8, 1969.

After dinner, they all headed back to Cielo Drive for a quiet evening. Roman was supposed to be back in Los Angeles the following week in anticipation of becoming a new father.

Sadly the story concludes here...

However....

In 2019 Quentin Tarentino created and directed an alternate history movie about the year 1969. It featured actors playing Sharon, Roman and Jay, along with other fictional characters. Rather than detailing the brutal reality of Sharon's last moments, Quentin added a satisfying twist at the end of the movie that made it extremely emotional for me. It brought tears to my eyes as I retell my story below. When the very eerie music and the credits came up on the screen and I left the theater, the only thing I was thinking was … *if only.*

Quentin Tarentino — autographed Pulp Fiction book.

Once upon a Time in Hollywood…..The Story

Once upon a Time in Hollywood is the fictional story created by writer-director Quentin Tarantino. It tells the story of Rick Dalton, an actor a little past his prime who was famous in the '50s for playing Jake Cahill, Bounty Hunter. Leonardo DiCaprio plays Dalton in the movie, and his character's long-time stunt man and friend Cliff Booth is played by Brad Pitt. The movie takes place in 1969, and also features real life characters including Sharon Tate, played by the lovely and beautiful Margot Robbie.

Going in, I didn't know what to expect from this movie — it was, after all, a Quentin Tarantino film. I am truly a fan of his work, but I know how his movies tend to end and was pretty nervous about what I'd be seeing. I had made a point of avoiding teasers, press coverage, etc. before going so that I didn't have any preconceived notions about it. Even though this was a DeCaprio/Pitt film, my focus was on Margot Robbie as Sharon. I believe in her brief scenes she stole the film by doing an amazing job of portraying Sharon's kindness and innocence, as well as showing the fun aspects of her life, especially at the Playboy Mansion dancing with her friends Mama Cass Elliott, Michelle Phillips and a brief but very strong performance by Damien Lewis) as Steve McQueen.

My favorite part of the movie is when Margot/Sharon is by herself on the streets of LA, picking up a strange hippie hitchhiker on Sunset Blvd. and showing her kindness by giving her a ride then later going to a bookstore to buy a book she ordered, the Thomas Hardy novel, *Tess of the d'Urbervilles.* Years later, Roman Polanski would direct the movie Tess, based upon Sharon's suggestions and ideas she had after reading that book. The other highlight, for me, was Sharon (Margot) seeing the film *The Wrecking Crew* with Dean Martin at the cinema. So she attends the film free of charge, once she introduces herself to the theater manager as "the actress from *Valley of the Dolls.*" She tells him she played Freya "the klutz" and he's more than happy to let her in for free.

What was really interesting is the real footage from the movie with Sharon and Dean Martin and later Nancy Kwan was shown, while you see her Margo/Sharon character and the audience enjoying the film. During the sequence, there are scenes where it shows Margot/Sharon practicing martial arts with Bruce Lee and recalling her time doing as she prepared her fight scenes for the movie with Kwan. Those scenes from the movie were very cool!

I still wasn't sure how Tarentino was going to handle Sharon's fate. They showed a very pregnant Sharon getting a visit from her friend, actress Joanna Pettet (played by Rumor Willis), and later Sharon with her friends Jay Sebring, Abigail Folger and Wojciech Frykowski at the Coyote restaurant. Then the scene with her friends at the piano, listening to music. By that time, I was getting nervous about how the film would end.

Much to my surprise, a series of strange and violent scenes were happening next door at Dalton's home, as the true fiction of the film unfolded. It was quiet and calm next door at Sharon's. It was then I realized why the film was titled the way it was. After all the craziness at Dalton's home, he sees Jay Sebring (played by Emile Hirsch) at the gate and they strike up a conversation that leads to seeing a young ,vibrant and very pregnant Sharon inviting Rick up to her home to meet her friends. When they walked up the long driveway together, it brought tears to my eyes. Tarentino, in true form, flipped the switch and rewrote history, allowing the theater audience to imagine what could have been, once upon a time.

Margot Robbie as Sharon hand signed photos from scenes in the movie.

In the movie *Once Upon a Time in Hollywood,* director Quentin Attention created an excellent soundtrack that took you back to 1969 and what was playing on the radio then. I was so knocked out by the movie, the music and the lyrics, I couldn't help singing to them afterwards. Here are a few images of the original 45 releases to bring to mind the lyrics and remind you of the movie.

"Blessed are they that mourn, for they shall be comforted." —St. Matt. V. 5.

Sacred Heart of Jesus
Have Mercy on the Soul of

SHARON TATE POLANSKI

Date of Death
August 9, 1969

PRAYER

O SWEETEST Heart of Jesus, ever present in the Blessed Sacrament, ever consumed with burning love for the captive souls in Purgatory, bring to the country of peace and light the Soul of Thy servant, whom Thou hast summoned to go forth from this world, and bid that Thy departed be numbered among Thy Saints, there to glorify Thee for ever and ever. Amen.

May the souls of all the faithful departed through the mercy of God, rest in peace. Amen.

Cunningham & O'Connor
Mortuaries

www.ingramcontent.com/pod-product-compliance
Lightning Source LLC
Chambersburg PA
CBHW061348010526
44107CB00011B/873